Summary of Contents

THE PRINCIPLES OF BEAUTIFUL WEB DESIGN

BY **JASON BEAIRD**
& JAMES GEORGE

The Principles of Beautiful Web Design

by Jason Beaird and James George

Copyright © 2014 SitePoint Pty. Ltd.

Product Manager: Simon Mackie   **Cover Design**: Alex Walker

Technical Editor: Giovanni DiFeterici

Editor: Paul Fitzpatrick

Printing History:

   First Edition: January 2007

   Second Edition: November 2010

   Third Edition: June 2014

Notice of Rights

Notice of Liability

The author and publisher have made every effort to ensure the accuracy of the information herein. However, the information contained in this book is sold without warranty, either express or implied. Neither the authors and SitePoint Pty Ltd, nor its dealers or distributors, will be held liable for any damages to be caused either directly or indirectly by the instructions contained in this book, or by the software or hardware products described herein.

Trademark Notice

Rather than indicating every occurrence of a trademarked name as such, this book uses the names only in an editorial fashion and to the benefit of the trademark owner, with no intention of infringement of the trademark.

Published by SitePoint Pty Ltd

Web: www.sitepoint.com

Email: business@sitepoint.com

ISBN 978-0-9922794-4-8

Printed and bound in the United States of America

About the Authors

Jason Beaird is a designer and front-end developer with over ten years of experience working on a wide range of award-winning web projects. With a background in graphic design and a passion for web standards, he's always looking for accessible ways to make the Web a more beautiful place. When he's not pushing pixels in Photoshop or tinkering with markup, Jason loves sharing his passion for the Web with others. He writes about his ideas, adventures, and random projects on his personal site, http://jasongraphix.com.

James George is a professional web designer from the United States, who is passionate about the field of design. He loves connecting with other designers and developers. James enjoys working closely with clients and businesses to create powerful, beautiful web design solutions. You can find him on Twitter[1], Google+[2], and LinkedIn[3].

About the Technical Editor

Giovanni DiFeterici is the Creative Director for the UnmatchedStyle brand and for Period-Three, a web design studio in Columbia, SC. He is the author of *The Web Designer's Roadmap* and an organizer for the ConvergeSE and BDConf web design conference series'. Recently, he cofounded SOCO[4], a relaxed coworking space for creatives, also in Columbia, SC. His goal is to make the web a more engaging and rewarding place to work and play. When he's not tinkering with code, you'll find him painting, running, and spending time with his lovely wife Amanda and their new son Roman.

About SitePoint

SitePoint specializes in publishing fun, practical, and easy-to-understand content for web professionals. Visit http://www.sitepoint.com/ to access our blogs, books, newsletters, articles, and community forums.

---

[1] https://twitter.com/creativebeacon/

[2] https://plus.google.com/u/0/+JamesGeorgeWebDesigner

[3] http://www.linkedin.com/in/creativepro

[4] http://soco-work.com/

Table of Contents

Chapter 2   Color 53

Preface

When my wife and I moved into our house, one of our first major projects was to update the bathroom. The horribly gaudy floral wallpaper pattern, along with the gold sink fixtures, obnoxious mirrors, and tacky lighting, made us feel like we'd stepped into a previous decade every time we entered the master bathroom. Removing wallpaper is a tough job, but it's even more difficult when there are multiple layers of the stuff. This was the case with our bathroom. Apparently the previous homeowners' taste in wallpaper changed every few years, and rather than stripping off the wallpaper and starting over, they just covered ugly with more ugly. Ah, the joys of home ownership!

If there's one thing our renovation adventures have taught me, it's that there are strong parallels between designing a room's decor and designing a good website.

Good design is about the relationships between the elements involved, and creating a balance between them.

Whether we're talking about a website or bathroom makeover, throwing up a new layer of wallpaper or changing the background color isn't a design solution in itself—it's just part of a solution. While we removed the wallpaper and rolled some paint onto our bathroom, we also had to change the light fixtures, remove the gold-trimmed shower doors, replace the mirrors, upgrade the lighting, paint the cabinets, change the switches and plugs, and scrape off the popcorn ceilings. If we'd just removed the tacky wallpaper and left all the other stuff, we'd still have an outdated bathroom. Website design is similar: you can only do so many minor updates before the time comes to scrap what you have and start over.

Fads come and go, but good design is timeless.

Conforming to the latest design trends is a good way to ensure temporary public appeal, but how long will those trends last? As far as I know, there was hardly ever a time when marquee and blink tags were accepted as professional web design markup ... but scrolling JavaScript news tickers, "high readability" hit-counters, and chunky table borders have graced the home pages of many high-profile sites in the past. These are the shag carpets, sparkly acoustic ceilings, and faux wood paneling of the web design world. Take a trip in the Internet Wayback Machine, and look for late-nineties versions of some of the top Fortune 500 and pre-dot-com boom-era websites. Try to find examples of good and bad design. In the midst of some of the most outdated, laughable websites, you're likely to find some pages that still look surprisingly relevant. Most likely, these designs aren't dependent on flashy Photoshop filters or trendy image treatments. As you read this book, keep in mind that good design transcends technology.

The finishing touches make a big impression.

I've heard it argued recently that deep down, people really love "anti-marketing design." The idea is that we trust sites that have an unpolished appearance and feel amateurish. I think this argument misses the point. No matter what type of website you're developing, the design should be as intentional as the functionality. My wife and I didn't change the functionality of our bathroom with the work that we did. We just fine-tuned the details, but it made a world of difference. Some people might have been able to live with the bathroom the way it was, but I doubt you'd find anyone who would say it was exactly what they wanted. Similarly, if you're spending time developing a website, you should take time to design it. Under no circumstances should the design feel unpolished or haphazard. If you want to come off as edgy, anti-marketing, and non-corporate, then do it, and do it well—but there's no reason to be ignorant about, or feel intimidated by, design.

My goal with this book is simple: to present what I know about designing for the Web in a way that anyone can understand and apply. Why? Because the basics of website design should be common knowledge. We all live in and work on an internet that has been blindly covering up ugly with more ugly since its inception. It's time to break that chain and make bold moves toward better design.

Who Should Read This Book

If you're squeamish about choosing colors, feel uninspired by a blank browser window, or get lost trying to choose the right font, this book is for you. I take a methodical approach to presenting traditional graphic design theory as it applies to today's website development industry. While the content is directed towards web programmers and developers, it provides a design primer and relevant examples that will benefit readers at any level.

What's in This Book

This book comprises the following five chapters. You can read them from beginning to end to gain a complete understanding of the subject, or skip around if you only need a refresher on a particular topic.

Chapter 1: *Layout and Composition*

An awareness of design relies heavily on understanding the spatial relationships that exist between the individual components of a design. The layout chapter kicks off the design process by investigating possible page components. With these blocks defined, we discuss some tools and examples that will help you start your own designs on a solid foundation. To wrap up this discussion, we'll examine Knoxville Reflexology, a real client project that we'll be following as an example through each chapter.

Chapter 2: *Color*

Perhaps the most mysterious aspect of design is the topic of color selection. Chapter 2 sheds light on this as we delve into both the aesthetic and scientific aspects of color theory. Armed with these simple guidelines, and some tips for creating harmonious color combinations, you'll see how anyone can choose a set of colors that work well together to complement the overall message of a website. Finally, we'll learn how the palette for Knoxville Reflexology was chosen.

Chapter 3: *Texture*

An aspect of web design that's often overlooked, texture is the key to creating designs that stand out. By understanding how the individual elements of texture function, you'll learn how to use points, lines, and shapes to communicate and support your site's message on a number of levels. We'll then get to see firsthand how subtle textures helped shape the identity and character of our example website.

Chapter 4: *Typography*

The importance of typography is undeniable. Type is everywhere, and understanding the mechanics of written language is essential for any visual designer. In this chapter, we'll dive beneath the surface of this rich topic, exploring the basics of the letterform, and investigating various typeface distinctions.

Chapter 5: *Imagery*

The necessary companions to any well-designed site are the images and illustrations that grace its pages. In the final chapter, we'll discuss what we should look for in the visual elements that we use on our pages, and locate sources of legitimate supporting imagery. Of course, finding the right image is often just the beginning. We'll also learn some image-editing basics before we see the final steps in our example project.

Conventions Used in This Book

You'll notice that we've used certain typographic and layout styles throughout the book to signify different types of information. Look out for the following items.

Code Samples

Code in this book will be displayed using a fixed-width font, like so:

```
<h1>A Perfect Summer's Day</h1>
<p>It was a lovely day for a walk in the park. The birds
were singing and the kids were all back at school.</p>
```

Some lines of code are intended to be entered on one line, but we've had to wrap them because of page constraints. A ➡ indicates a line break that exists for formatting purposes only, and should be ignored:

```
URL.open("http://www.sitepoint.com/blogs/2007/05/28/user-style-she
➡ets-come-of-age/");
```

Tips, Notes, and Warnings

Hey, You!

Tips will give you helpful little pointers.

Ahem, Excuse Me ...

Notes are useful asides that are related—but not critical—to the topic at hand. Think of them as extra tidbits of information.

Make Sure You Always ...

... pay attention to these important points.

Watch Out!

Warnings will highlight any gotchas that are likely to trip you up along the way.

Supplementary Materials

http://www.learnable.com/books/the-principles-of-beautiful-web-design/
The book's website, containing links, updates, resources, and more.

http://www.sitepoint.com/forums/forumdisplay.php?53-CSS-amp-Page-Layout
SitePoint's forums, for help on any tricky web problems.

books@sitepoint.com
Our email address, should you need to contact us for support, to report a problem, or for any other reason.

Want to Take Your Learning Further?

Thanks for buying this book. We appreciate your support. Do you want to continue learning? You can now get unlimited access to courses and ALL SitePoint books at Learnable for one low price. Enroll now and start learning today! Join Learnable and you'll stay ahead of the newest technology trends: http://www.learnable.com.

Layout and Composition

For many web developers, myself included, the most intimidating part of the design process is getting started. Imagine for a moment that you're sitting at your desk with nothing other than a cup of coffee and the business card of a potential client who needs a basic corporate website. Usually, a business card speaks volumes about a company's identity, and can be used as design inspiration.

Unfortunately, that's not the case with the card for Smith's Services in Figure 1.1. It's black and white, all text, no character—blah. Talk about a blank canvas! So, where do you go from here? You need a plan... and you need to contact Mr. Smith. With some critical input from the client about what his company actually does, and by gathering information about the content you have to work with, you'll be able to come up with a successful design.

SMITH'S SERVICES

Jim Smith
Professional Service Associate

100 Random Street
Suite 16
Somewhere, VA 54321

Tel. 867-5309
Fax. 555-2368

Figure 1.1. A bland client business card

Anyone, no matter what level of artistic talent, can come up with a design that works well and looks good—all it takes is a little experience and a working knowledge of some basic layout principles. So let's start with the basics, and before long you'll have the foundation necessary to design gallery-quality websites.

The Design Process

Designing a website can be a double-edged sword. The process falls somewhere between art, science, and problem solving. Yes, we want to create an individual site that's aesthetically pleasing, but our highest priority should be to meet the needs of our client. These needs may be lofty and elaborate, or they might just be about making information available. If we fail to listen carefully, though, the entire project will come falling down, along with our reputation. The technical details of developing, hosting, and maintaining a website or application can be, well, technical. The process of creating a design comp, however, can be boiled down to just three key tasks: discovery, exploration, and implementation.

 What's a Comp?

The word **comp** is an abbreviation of the phrase "comprehensive dummy"—a term that comes from the print design world. It's a complete simulation of a printed layout that's created before the layout goes to press. In translating this term to web design, a comp is an image of a layout that's created before we begin to prototype the design in HTML.

Discovery

The discovery component of the design process is about meeting the clients and learning what they do. This may feel a little counter-intuitive, but gathering information about who your clients are and how they run their business is vital in coming up with an appropriate and effective design.

Before you schedule your first meeting with a client, spend some time researching their business. If they've asked you to design a website, they may currently be without one, but google them anyway. If you're unable to find any information about their business specifically, try to learn as much as you can about their industry before the first meeting. Whenever possible, the first meeting with a client should be conducted in person. Sometimes, distance will dictate that the meeting has to occur over the phone; but if the client is in town, schedule a time to meet face-to-face.

Keep in mind that this meeting is less about impressing the client, selling yourself, or selling a website than it is about communication and establishing just what it is the client wants. Try to listen more than you speak, and bring a pad of paper on which you can make notes. If you bring a laptop or tablet with you to talk about website examples, limit the time spent using it. Computers have screens, and people tend to stare at them; and so, if the client isn't staring at the screen the whole time, you're likely to be as you write your notes. If you must drag some technology into the meeting, use a voice recording app to record the conversation—with the client's permission, of course. In my experience, though, a pad of paper is less threatening and far less distracting to the often not-so-tech-savvy client.

 Client Meetings Don't Have to Take Place in an Office

Even when I worked for a company in a big office, I had some of my most productive client meetings at a café or over lunch. The feasibility of this approach depends on the client. If your contact seems to be more the formal business type, don't suggest it; in many cases, though, it's a good way to make a business meeting more personal.

Here are a few of the questions I like to ask in initial client meetings, even if I've already established the answer myself via a search engine:

- What does the company do?
- What is your role in the company?[1]
- Does the company have an existing logo or brand? What is your goal in developing a website?
- What information do you wish to provide online?
- Who comprises your target audience? Do its members share any common demographics, like age, sex, or a physical location?
- Who are your competitors and do they have websites?
- Do you have examples of websites you like or dislike?
- What kind of timeline do you have for the project and what is the budget?

If the project is to redesign an existing website, I also like to ask:

- What are your visitors usually looking for when they come to your site?
- What are the problems with your current design?
- What do you hope to achieve with a redesign?
- Are there any elements of the current site that you want to keep?
- How do you think your visitors will react to a new site design?

Sometimes I start off with more questions than those listed here. Use your imagination and try to come up with some creative queries that will really give you more insight into the client's organization. If you're a programmer, avoid the tech jargon. If you're a designer, avoid talking specifically about design. Sure, that may be all you're thinking about, but semantic markup, responsive layouts, and so on will likely mean very little to the client. Worse still, these types of conversations can bring misguided design opinions your way before you have a chance to start thinking about the design yourself.

---

[1] This question is especially important if this person is going to be your main point of contact.

Exploration

The next stage of the design process is to take the information you've learned from the client back to your laboratory for analysis, dissection, and experimentation. You want to develop a firm grasp on all the information, products, and services they have to offer, and play around with how these could be arranged. Put yourself in the shoes of the website visitors and ask yourself what these people are looking for. If you're thinking about buying a product, what do you need to know before you buy? If you're signing up for a service, where would you learn about the different offerings and which level of service you need? What is the clearest title possible for page x, and how many steps does it take to reach page y?

In the world of web design, this is the beginning of a process known as **information architecture**, or IA for short. For expansive websites and complex web applications, information architecture is a career in itself, but the guiding principles of this field can provide a solid foundation for even the smallest websites. For the exploration stage of our process, we want to focus on organizing the content and flow of the website into a structure we can design around.

Two of the most essential tools for this task are scrap paper (or a whiteboard if you have one) and a big pad of sticky notes. Make a list of all the bits and pieces of the website and start arranging them into groups and subgroups. These are likely to move around quite a bit, and that's where the sticky notes come in handy. If you make a note for every section, subsection, and page of the site, you can arrange them on a wall in the order they'll appear in your site's navigation. You'll want to avoid overwhelming the visitors with too many options, but you also don't want to bury information too deeply within the site; that is, too many clicks away from the home page. There are no hard-and-fast rules for this activity; just make the information as obvious and as easy to reach as possible.

Implementation

Now that we've thought through how we want to organize the information we're working with, the implementation step of our design process begins with creating a layout. Regardless of the project, try to avoid being caught up in the technology associated with building websites—at least at first. At this point, it's unimportant whether the site is going to comprise straight HTML, a template for a content management system, or a Ruby on Rails application; the bottom line is that we have an interface to design and a blank sheet of paper. "Paper?" That's right, paper. Did you really think I was going to let you go back to your precious computer already? No way. Here's why: it's easy to lose focus on the design if you start thinking about the layout in front of a computer. If you start out on paper, you can ignore the technical limitations of browsers and CSS, and focus on how you want the final product to look. Now you might think that all good designers carry around fancy hard-bound sketch books in which they flourish expensive markers and paintbrushes to design Da Vinci-esque renderings of potential web page layouts. For my part, I use a 79-cent spiral-bound notebook and any writing instrument I can find on my desk that still works.

I start out by sketching a few possible layouts. After I've produced a few, I decide on one I like, jump into Photoshop, and use the rectangle tool to block out the areas I've marked down on my paper. Once I've defined my layout, I experiment with foreground and background colors until I have a solid color scheme. I continue twiddling the Photoshop knobs and pushing around pixels until, finally, magically, I have a comp to show the client.

Simple, right? Okay, perhaps I skipped a few steps in that brief description. Honestly, though, when people ask me how I do what I do, they usually receive a similar explanation. The truth is that there are reams of now-subconscious information from my past experience and those old college design and art classes that have helped me to define my own design process.

Learning how to design is like learning how to program. Some people have a bit of a knack for it, but anyone can learn. Just as there's good code and ugly code, there is good design and ugly design. Learning some of the principles and conventions associated with design will help you to understand the difference between the good, the bad, and the ugly, moving you towards establishing your own design process.

Defining Good Design

There are two main standpoints from which most people determine whether a website design is "good" or "bad." There's a strict usability angle, which focuses on functionality, the effective presentation of information, and efficiency. Then there's the purely aesthetic perspective, which is all about the artistic value and visual appeal of the design. Some people become caught up in the aesthetics and graphics, and forget about the user, while some usability gurus get lost in their user testing and forget about visual appeal. In order to reach people and retain their interest, it's essential to maximize both.

The most important point to keep in mind is that design is about communication. If you create a website that works and presents information well, but looks ugly or fails to fit with the client's brand, no one will want to use it. Similarly, if you make a beautiful website that is hard to use or inaccessible, people will leave. Indeed, the elements and functionality of a finished website design should work as a single cohesive unit, so that:

Users are pleased by the design but drawn to the content

One of the biggest concerns among usability professionals is the time it takes users to scan the page for the information they want, be it a piece of content, a link to another page, or a form field. The design should not be a hindrance; it should act as a conduit between the user and the information.

Harmony Republic[2] (pictured in Figure 1.2) is a great example of a design that's both beautiful and usable. The richly textured, colorful illustrations flow around the structure of the page, which is embellished with hand-drawn navigation and a simple layout. The abundance of

---

[2] http://www.harmonyrepublic.com/

handcrafted, organic elements creates contrast and helps to draw your eyes to the featured artists without interfering with the pages' readability or how it's organized.

Figure 1.2. Harmony Republic

Users can move about easily via intuitive navigation

We'll talk more about the placement of navigation later, but the main navigation block itself should be clearly visible on the page, and each link should have a descriptive title. A navigation structure that not only changes appearance when hovered over with the cursor, but also indicates the active page or section (as the menu shown in Figure 1.3 does), helps users to recognize where they are, and how to get where they want to go.

Figure 1.3. A navigation menu from nclud.com, a Washington, DC-based web design agency

Secondary navigation, search fields, and outgoing links should not be dominant features of the page. If we make these items easy to find, and separate them visually from the content, we allow users to focus on the information—yet they'll know where to look when they're ready to move on to other content.

Users recognize each page as belonging to the site

Even if there's a dramatic difference between the layout of the home page and the rest of the site, a cohesive theme or style should exist across all site pages to help hold the design together.

Take a look at the three screenshots from the Moore School of Business website[3] in Figure 1.4. Although the content blocks on these pages are divided differently, there are several visual indicators that let users know that these are pages from the same site. Much of this unity is due to the repetition of the identity and navigation blocks. The consistent use of a very limited color palette (black, gray, yellow, and red) also helps to unify the pages.

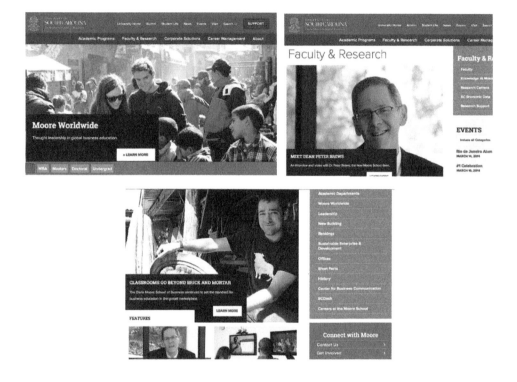

Figure 1.4. Pages from the Moore School of Business

---

[3] http://mooreschool.sc.edu/

Web Page Anatomy

Even from a non-designer's standpoint, defining a design that satisfies all the requirements I outlined above is a simple task. It's similar to making a phrase on your refrigerator with magnetic poetry words. Although there are millions of ways to arrange the words, only a few arrangements make any sense. The magnetic words are like the components, or blocks, of the web page. Although the number of these necessary blocks depends on the size and subject of the site, most websites have the components seen in Figure 1.5.

Figure 1.5. Anatomy of a website

Let's look at each of these components in turn:

Containing block

Every web page has a container. This could be in the form of the page's body tag, an all-containing div tag. Without some sort of container, we'd have no place to put the contents of our page. The elements would drift beyond the bounds of our browser window and off into empty space. The width of this container can be fluid, meaning that it expands to fill the width of browser window; or fixed, so that the content is the same width no matter what size the window is.

Logo

When designers refer to an identity, they're referring to the logo and colors that exist across a company's various forms of marketing, such as business cards, letterhead, brochures, and so on.[4] The identity block that appears on the website should contain the company's logo or name, and sit at the top of each page of the website. The identity block increases brand recognition while informing users that the pages they're viewing are part of a single site.

Navigation

It's essential that the site's navigation system is easy to find and use. Users expect to see navigation right at the top of the page. Whether you plan to use vertical menus down the side of the page, or a horizontal menu across the page, the navigation should be as close to the top of the layout as possible. At the very least, all main navigation items should appear "above the fold."

 Above the Fold

The **fold**, as many designers call it, is where the content of a page ends before users scroll down. This metaphor is derived from the fold in a newspaper. If you look at the cover of a folded newspaper, most of the headlines and biggest news appear in the top half, so that the most important news items can be seen at a glance when the newspaper is folded. The location of the fold on a web page depends on the browser dimensions and the user's screen resolution.

Content

Content is king. Content consists of any text, images, or videos found on a website. A typical website visitor will enter and leave a website in a matter of seconds. If visitors are unable to find what they're looking for, they'll undoubtedly close the browser or move on to another site. It's important to keep the main content block as the focal point of a design, so that visitors can scan the page for the information they need.

Footer

Located at the bottom of the page, the footer usually contains copyright, contact, and legal information, as well as a few links to the main sections of the site. By separating the end content from the bottom of the browser window, the footer should indicate to users that they're at the bottom of the page.

Whitespace

The graphic design term whitespace (or negative space) literally refers to any area of a page without type or illustrations. While many novice web designers (and most clients) feel a need to fill every inch of a web page with photos, text, tables, and data, empty space on a page is every bit as important as having content. Without carefully planned whitespace, a design will

---

[4] Many people use the words "identity" and "branding" interchangeably. Branding is a broad term that describes the process of developing an awareness of a company, product, or service. The branding process involves advertising, market research, customer feedback, and much more. Identity is actually a subset of branding in that it deals only with the visual aspects of branding.

feel closed in, like a crowded room. Whitespace helps a design to *breathe* by guiding the user's eye around a page, but also helps to create balance and unity—two important concepts that we'll discuss in more detail later in this chapter.

At this point, we've had our initial meeting with Mr. Smith, our theoretical client, and it was helpful. He explained very thoroughly what his business does and what he wants the site to achieve. Even though we've yet to see actual content, we can use the standard blocks of web page anatomy to start developing a layout. Although other site-specific blocks are worked into the designs of many website layouts, the web page anatomy works to summarize the most common blocks.

Now that we have this information, how can we use it to create a foundational layout for Smith's Services? It's time for some grid theory.

Grid Theory

When most people think about grids, they think about engineering and architecture. However, the grid is an essential tool for graphic design as well, and the use of grids in website design have exploded in popularity in the last few years.

Using a grid is more than simply making elements on the page square and lined up: it's about proportion as well. That's where the theory comes into grid theory. Many art historians credit Dutch painter Piet Mondrian as the father of graphic design for his sophisticated use of grids. Yet classical grid theory has influenced successful artistic efforts for thousands of years. The concept of dividing the elements of a composition extends back to the mathematical ideas established by Pythagoras and his followers, who defined numbers as ratios rather than single units.

The Pythagoreans observed a mathematical pattern that occurred so often in nature that they believed it to be divinely inspired. They referred to this pattern as the golden ratio or divine proportion. The basic idea is illustrated in Figure 1.6.

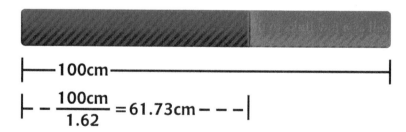

Figure 1.6. The golden ratio

A line can be bisected using the golden ratio by dividing its length by 1.62. This magical 1.62 number is really 1.6180339 …, an irrational number that's usually represented as Φ (pronounced "phi"). Explaining the math used to come up with this number is a bit too involved for this discussion, and is likely to be of no real help to you becoming a better designer, so I'll spare you the details. Besides, my math is a little rusty.

So just what does this ratio have to do with graphic design? In general, compositions divided by lines that are proportionate to the golden ratio are considered to be aesthetically pleasing. The artists of the Renaissance used divine proportion to design their paintings, sculpture, and architecture, just as designers today often employ this ratio when creating page layouts, posters, and brochures. Rather than relying on artistic notion, divine proportion gives us logical guidelines for producing appealing layouts.

This sunflower is an example of the golden ratio in nature, as Figure 1.7 shows. The diameter of the sunflower's center is the total diameter of the sunflower, including the petals, divided by Φ.

Figure 1.7. The golden ratio in nature

The Rule of Thirds

A simplified version of the golden ratio is the rule of thirds. A line bisected by the golden ratio is divided into two sections, one of which is approximately twice the size of the other. Dividing a composition into thirds is an easy way to apply divine proportion without your calculator.

For quick layout experimentation, I like to start off by drawing a bunch of simple rule-of-thirds grids with pencil and paper. Just draw a rectangle, divide it into thirds horizontally and vertically, then draw a line between each vertical line to create six columns to work within, as shown in Figure 1.8.

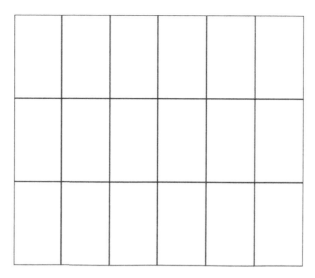

Figure 1.8. A simple grid

With this simple gridwork in place, we can begin to lay out our elements. This is often referred to as a **wireframe**. Wireframes are simple sketches or layouts where you design blocks of content and their positioning on the page. Wireframes are extremely useful, because you can quickly and easily move elements around. The largest, outermost rectangle represents the container that we talked about in the section called "Web Page Anatomy". When using this method of layout design, I like to place the biggest block first. Usually, that block represents the content. In my first rule-of-thirds grid, I place the content block within the two-thirds of the layout at the lower-right. Next, I place my navigation block in the middle third of the left-hand column. I place the text part of the identity block over the left side of the content, and the image part of the identity over the menu. Finally, I squash the copyright block below the content, in the right-hand column of the grid. The result is the top-left of the four possible layout arrangements shown in Figure 1.9.

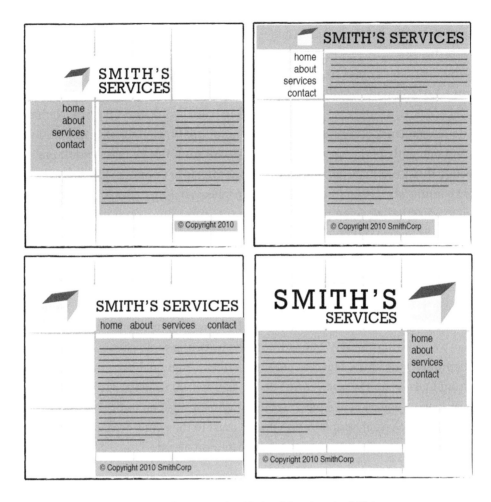

Figure 1.9. Four layouts in grids that follow the rule of thirds

These initial sketches provide a quick look into what general layout approaches might work for your website. No need to stop there, though—the growth in popularity of grid-based design on the Web has inspired many great articles about—and tools for—designing websites on a grid.

960 Grid System

One of my favorite tools for laying out website components is the set of templates and sketch sheets from Nathan Smith's 960 Grid System.[5] Inspired by articles from web designers Khoi Vinh and Mark Boulton, the 960 Grid System is primarily a CSS framework.

 CSS Frameworks

A CSS framework is a CSS system that is set up to handle the grid structure of a website. Common CSS frameworks are based on 12 column, 18 column, or 24 column layouts. The reason these

---

[5] http://960.gs/

numbers are chosen is because they offer the most combinations of multiple column widths, since these numbers are divisible by 1, 2, 3, 4, and 6.

The width of the templates comes from an article by Cameron Moll. In contemplating what width would fit within 1,024px wide displays, Moll landed at 960px, and pointed out that the number was divisible by 3, 4, 5, 6, 8, 10, 12, 15, and 16—making it an ideal width for grids. Nathan combined these ideas into a framework and created three layout foundations: one with 12 columns, one with 16 columns, and one with 24. I personally prefer to work from the 12-column templates, as they allow me to easily divide content into quarters by spanning four columns, thirds by spanning three, and halves by spanning six. Using these sketch sheets makes it easy to transition from your sketches and mock-ups to an actual working prototype. Note that this approach translates well to many other popular CSS frameworks as well, such as Foundation[6] and Bootstrap[7], because they are also based on 12-column grids—we'll discuss Bootstrap and Foundation in more detail a little later.

As you experiment with different arrangements for your own layouts, use the columns of whatever grid you've chosen as alignment guides for the identity, navigation, content, and footer blocks. It's very tempting to arrange all your elements within the same one or two blocks, but try to avoid this—it's not very interesting visually. Instead, consider pushing some elements into another column or off the grid entirely. One of the biggest complaints new designers have about working with grids is that everything looks boxed in and *griddy*. To those opposed to using grids for this reason, I say take a look at websites such as 10K Apart,[8] seen in Figure 1.10. The red columns you see are from the 16-column 960 Grid System template, and do not exist in the actual website. With those columns hidden, you might never realize this design was created on a grid.

To quote Josef Müller-Brockmann, graphic design pioneer (and author of *Grid Systems in Graphic Design*): "The grid system is an aid, not a guarantee. It permits a number of possible uses and each designer can look for a solution appropriate to his personal style. But one must learn how to use the grid; it is an art that requires practice."[9]

---

[6] http://foundation.zurb.com/

[7] http://getbootstrap.com/

[8] http://10k.aneventapart.com/

[9] Josef Müller-Brockmann, *The Graphic Artist and His Design Problems*, Arthur Niggli Ltd, Switzerland, 1961, p 92

Figure 1.10. 10K Apart website with 16-column grid overlay

The longing we have for structure, grids, and ideal proportion is deeply ingrained in human nature. A layout that "doesn't look quite right" can often be fixed by moving elements and resizing them on the grid. So if a layout isn't working, keep experimenting. At some point, all the pieces will click together and the Tetris level-up sound will play in your head. You will have achieved balance.

Balance

In a figurative sense, the concept of **visual balance** is similar to that of physical balance illustrated by a seesaw. Just as physical objects have weight, so do the elements of a layout. If the elements on either side of a layout are of equal weight, they balance one another. There are two main forms of visual balance: symmetrical and asymmetrical.

Symmetrical Balance

Figure 1.11. Examples of symmetrical balance

Symmetrical balance, or formal balance, occurs when the elements of a composition are the same on either side of an axis line, as shown in Figure 1.11. The digital painting *Contemplation* by David Lanham, shown in Figure 1.12, illustrates this concept well. Notice how the male and female figures are similar in position and proportion. Even the shaded background boxes are mirror images of one another.

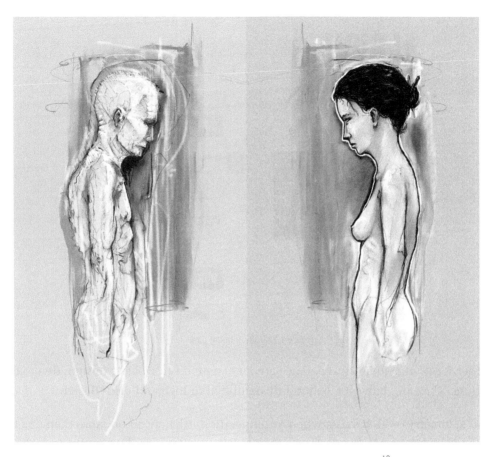

Figure 1.12. Symmetrical balance: *Contemplation* by David Lanham[10]

Although it may not be practical for all designs and clients, this type of symmetry—called **horizontal symmetry**—can be applied to website layouts by centering content or balancing it between columns. The Albion West Coast page[11] is an example of such symmetry. Notice on the screenshot in Figure 1.13 that the content areas are balanced in perfect symmetry, While some elements, like the hand-drawn sketch in the background, add subtle variation to the site.

---

[10] http://dlanham.com/
[11] http://www.albionwestcoast.com/

Figure 1.13. Albion home page

The two other forms of symmetrical balance are less common in website design, due to the nature of the medium. They are, however, commonly exhibited in logo and print design:

- **bilateral symmetry**, which exists when a composition is balanced on more than one axis
- **radial symmetry**, which occurs when elements are equally spaced around a central point

Asymmetrical Balance

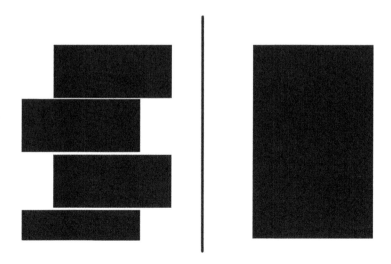

Figure 1.14. An example of asymmetrical balance

Asymmetrical balance, or informal balance, is a little more abstract (and more visually interesting in general) than symmetrical balance. An example of asymmetrical balance is shown in Figure 1.14. Rather than mirror images on either side of the layout, asymmetrical balance involves objects of differing size, shape, tone, or placement. These objects are arranged so that, despite their differences, they equalize the weight of the page; for instance, if you have a large object on one side of a page, and partner it with several smaller items on the other side, the composition can still feel balanced.

The concert poster by my friend Jeremy Darty presented in Figure 1.15 is a fine example of asymmetrical balance. The visual weight of the large pink flamingo on the left is balanced by the combined weight of the smaller flamingos and text blocks on the right-hand side of the layout. Notice, also, Jeremy's use of the rule of thirds. The blue cloud behind the Pop Sucks title takes up one-third of the vertical space and spans two-thirds of the horizontal.

Figure 1.15. Asymmetrically balanced design by Jeremy Darty

Take a look at the photo of the three stones in Figure 1.16. It may not be a particularly exciting picture, but as far as balance goes, it rocks! If you were to use a piece of paper to cover any one of the three stones below, the entire photograph would feel unbalanced and unfinished. This is generally the way balance works. It's as if the entire composition is in a picture frame hanging by a single nail on the wall. It barely takes much weight on one side or the other to shift the entire picture off balance.

Figure 1.16. Asymmetrical rocks that don't roll

Unlike symmetrical balance, asymmetrical balance is versatile and, as such, is used more often on the Web. If you take a look at most two-column website layouts, you'll notice that the wider column is often lighter in color—a tactic that creates a good contrast for the text and main content. The diminutive navigational column is often darker, has some sort of border, or is made to stand out in another way, in order to create balance within the layout. The About Us page of the Steinway & Sons website,[12] shown in Figure 1.17, is an excellent example of asymmetrical balance. In this example, there's no defined right column, just a large stoic image of the company's founder. That epic moustache carries a lot of weight, but it's balanced out by the sizeable italic headline atop the main content.

---

[12] http://www.steinway.com/about/

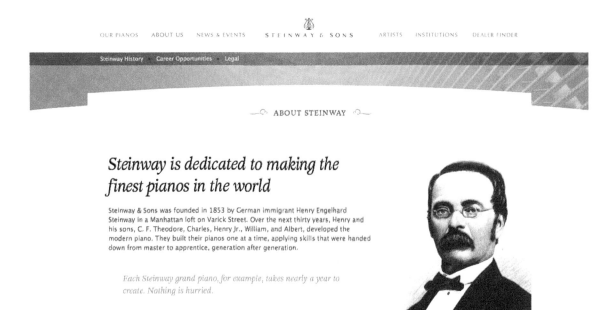

Figure 1.17. Steinway & Sons—an example of asymmetrical balance

There are many other principles at work in Jesse Bennet Chamberlain's design of the Steinway & Sons site, and it goes beyond asymmetrical balance. The site has great harmony,[13] which comes from the repeated use of curves, textures, and consistent typefaces. Much of that harmony can be explained via the principles of unity.

Unity

Design theory describes unity as the way in which the different elements of a composition interact with one another. A unified layout is one that works as a whole rather than being identified as separate pieces. Take the monkeys in Figure 1.18, for example. Their similarity of shape (not to mention their identical color) enables them to be recognized as a group, rather than four disparate elements.

---

[13] No pun intended.

Figure 1.18. Unity among the monkeys

Although less of an issue these days, unity is one of the many reasons why web designers have always despised HTML frames. It's important that unity exists not only within each element of a web page, but across the entire web page—the page itself must work as a unit. We can use a couple of approaches to achieve unity in a layout (aside from avoiding frames): proximity and repetition.

Proximity

Proximity is an obvious, but often overlooked, way to make a group of objects feel like a single unit. Placing objects close together within a layout creates a focal point towards which the eye will gravitate. Take a look at the digital painting in Figure 1.19. While composed of a seemingly random assortment of strokes, the five strokes that are the closest to each other appear to form a unified object.

Figure 1.19. Creating a group using proximity

We practice the concept of proximity on the Web when we start setting margins and padding for elements. For instance, when I define the CSS style rules for sites, I usually change the default margin that exists between common HTML elements such as headings (h1, h2, h3 …), paragraphs, blockquotes, and even images. By altering these values, I can cause more or less space to appear between elements, thereby creating groups.

If you look at the two columns of text in Figure 1.20, you'll notice that they look similar. The only difference is in the placement of the headings. In the column on the left, the word "Unkgnome" is equidistant from the top and bottom paragraphs. The result is that it looks more like a separator than a heading for the next paragraph. In the second column, the "Gnomenclature" heading is placed closer to the paragraph that follows it. In accordance with the rules of proximity, this heading appears to belong to that block of text.

Figure 1.20. Proximity between headers and content

Repetition

A gaggle of geese, a school of fish, a pride of lions. Any time you bring a set of like items together, they form a group. In the same way, repetition of colors, shapes, textures, or similar objects helps to tie a web page design together so that it feels like a cohesive unit. The example in Figure 1.21 illustrates repetition. Even though there exists other similar strokes, the nine red strokes on the left-hand side appear to be a unified group because they repeat a shape, color, and texture. The strokes to the right of this group have no repeated pattern, so they appear isolated even though there are other shapes nearby.

Figure 1.21. Creating a group using repetition

Whether you notice it or not, repetition is often used in website designs to unify elements of the layout. An example of this concept at work among unmodified HTML elements is the bulleted list. The bullet that precedes each list item is a visual indicator that the bullet items are parts of a whole.

Repeated patterns and textures can also help to unify a design. Take a look at the screenshot of Dribbble[14], a hub for designers and developers to showcase and share their work. This layout contains many eye-catching elements, but the repeated thumbnail images with the views, comments & like icons create a sense of unity, while the navigation bar and the open content area give plenty of room to show off all of this awesome, unique design work.

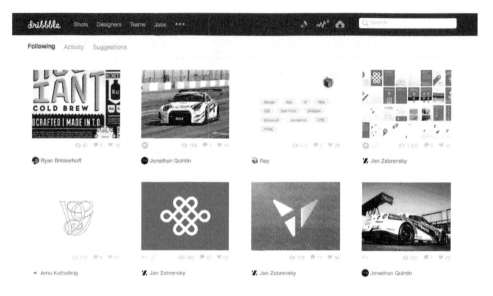

Figure 1.22. Dribbble homepage

Emphasis

Closely related to the idea of unity is the concept of emphasis or dominance. Rather than focusing on the various elements of a design fitting together, emphasis is about making a particular feature draw the viewer's attention. When you design a web page layout, often you'll identify an item in the content, or the layout itself, that you want to stand out. Perhaps it's a button for users to press, or an error message for them to read. One method of achieving such emphasis is by making that element into a focal point. A **focal point** is any element on a page that draws the viewer's eye, rather than just being part of the page as a whole or blending in with its surroundings. As with unity, there are a few tried-and-true methods of achieving a focal point.

Placement

Although the constraints of practical web design do not often allow for it, the direct center of a composition is the point at which users look first, and is typically the strongest location for producing emphasis. The further from the center an element is, the less likely it will be noticed first. On the Web, the top-left corner of the page also tends to demand a lot of attention for those of us who read from left to right (remember that many languages, like Hebrew and Arabic, are read from right to left) and scan a page from top to bottom.

---

[14] https://dribbble.com/

Continuance

The idea behind **continuance** or **flow** is that when our eyes start moving in one direction, they tend to continue along that path until a more dominant feature comes along. Figure 1.23 demonstrates this effect. Even though the bottom splotch is bigger and so tends to catch your eye first, your brain can't help but go "Hey, looky there, an arrow!" Soon enough, you'll find yourself staring at the smaller object.

Figure 1.23. Continuance and placement: creating emphasis

Continuance is one of the most common methods that web designers use to unify a layout. By default, the left edge of headings, copy, and images placed on a web page form a vertical line down the left side of a page before any styling is applied. A simple way to make additional use of this concept is to align elements to the lines of your grid. This creates multiple lines of continuance for your visitors' eyes to follow down the page. The example in Figure 1.24 below, the site of graphic designer Arnuad Beelen,[15] is a great example of continuance. The angled images align their edges with the tops or bottoms of others, moving your eye across the page.

---

[15] http://www.arnaudbeelen.be/

Figure 1.24. Continuance on Arnaud Beelen's site

Isolation

In the same way that proximity helps us create unity in a design, isolation promotes emphasis. An item that stands out from its surroundings will tend to demand attention. Even though he's sad to be apart from his buddies, the isolated monkey in Figure 1.25 stands out as a focal point on the page.

Figure 1.25. Isolation: a sad monkey

Contrast

Contrast is defined as the juxtaposition of dissimilar graphic elements, and is the most common method used to create emphasis in a layout. The concept is simple: the greater the difference between a graphic element and its surroundings, the more that element will stand out. Contrast can be created using differences in color (which I'll discuss in more detail in Chapter 2), size, and shape. Take a look at the Twitter home page in Figure 1.26.

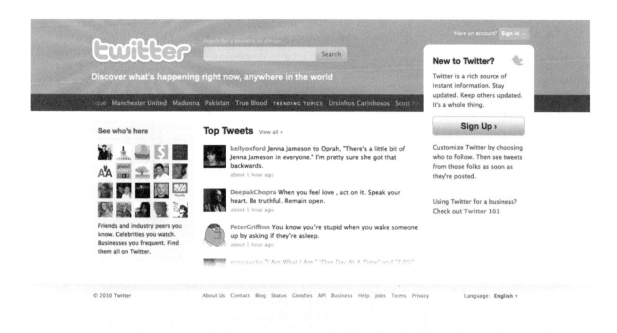

Figure 1.26. Twitter: using orange for contrast

If there's a singular link or button you want your visitors to click on in a page, it's known as a **call to action**. When you look at the preceding layout, what first grabs your attention? For me, it's the **Sign Up** button in the right column. It's the only place on the page that uses those bright orange and yellow colors, and the text is much bigger than the **Search** and **Sign In** buttons. By placing it in a block that crosses over that trending topics bar, it has plenty of continuance, isolation, and contrast. Twitter really wants you to click that button, so it's creating as much emphasis as possible to ensure its call to action is effective.

Proportion

Another interesting way of creating emphasis in a composition is through the use of proportion. Proportion is a principle of design that has to do with differences in the scale of objects. If we place an object in an environment that's of smaller scale than the object itself, that object will appear larger than it does in real life, and vice versa. This difference in proportion draws viewers' attention to the object, as it seems out of place in that context.

In Figure 1.27, I've taken our sad, isolated monkey and superimposed him over the skyline of Manhattan to prove my point. Between the sharp contrast in color and the difference in proportion, your brain immediately says, "Hey, this isn't quite right," and you're left staring at the monkey until you force yourself to look away.

Figure 1.27. Proportion: a monkey in Manhattan

This principle works for miniaturization as well. Take a look at the Barley's Greenville website[16] in Figure 1.28. The first element you probably notice is the massive Barley's header. From here, though, my eye jumps straight to the logo and into the row mentioning the menu and their beer selection. This is due to both continuance and eye-catching use of proportion. The proportions aren't true to life, because the beer is larger than the pizza, but the layout still works well and holds your attention.

---

[16] http://www.barleysgville.com/

Figure 1.28. Barley's: a great example of emphasis

Creating emphasis in your design isn't just the key to making your call to action stand out. It's also how we move a viewer's eyes across the page. By giving elements a descending level of emphasis, you can suggest an order for visitors to follow. If you keep this in mind as you build your sites, you can echo the emphasis you create with semantic HTML markup and CSS. For instance, by matching h1 to h6 headline tags with a respective level of visual emphasis, you can provide a similar view of what's visually important in the page to search engines and vision-impaired visitors.

Next, we'll look at some well-tested examples of designs from which you can work.

Bread-and-butter Layouts

Most of what we've talked about thus far has been design theory. Theory's helpful, but it can only take us so far towards understanding why some ideas work—and others don't—in a website's design. In my opinion, examples and practice are much more valuable. Most academic graphic design programs include a curriculum that's rich in art history and fine art. These classes provide a great foundation for an understanding of graphic design from an art perspective, but they do little to prepare you for the specific challenges you encounter when you take your designs to the Web.

Pablo Picasso once said, "I am always doing that which I cannot do, in order that I may learn how to do it." While I like to take that approach when designing a new website, it's important first to know what you can do. When you look out across the Internet, you can see that the possibilities for layout are endless. Depending on the goals of the site, though, only a few of those possibilities make good design sense. That's why we see certain configurations of identity, navigation, and content over and over again.

In this section, we'll talk about the three most common layouts, and explore some of their advantages and disadvantages.

Left-column Navigation

Regardless of whether we're talking about liquid or fixed-width layout design, the left-column navigation format is a time-honored standard. The layout of the Arbor Restaurant Site[17] pictured in Figure 1.29, is a classic example of this configuration. Many sites that fit into this mold don't necessarily use the left column as the main navigation block—sometimes you'll see the navigation along the top of the page—but they still divide the layout below the header into a narrow (one-third or less) left column and a wide right column. It's like a security blanket, or that comfortable shirt with holes in the armpits that you wear once a week—even though it drives your spouse crazy. For those reasons, a layout featuring left-column navigation is a safe choice for most projects.

Figure 1.29. Left-column navigation at Arbor

The downside to sites that use left-column navigation is that they can appear to lack creativity. It's been done so many times, in so many ways, over so many years that these sites tend to look the same. That's not to say you should avoid using a left-column navigation layout. At a guess, I'd say that 75% of the sites I've designed have a secondary left-column navigation, but I do try to mix it up a little when I can.

Speaking of mixing it up, how about picking that left column up and sticking it on the other side of the content? Then you'd have a right-column navigation layout.

Right-column Navigation

If you're going to restrict your main content to one side of the page, it's more widespread these days to push it to the left, placing navigation, advertising, and subsidiary content on the right. This is

---

[17] http://www.arbor-restaurant.co.uk/

an especially common configuration for news sites, social networks, and websites with expansive navigation schemes that are unable to be contained within a simple top navigation. BlueCross BlueShield of South Carolina[18] is an example of such a site. It features several different layouts and color schemes for each section. The screenshot you see in Figure 1.30 is a fourth-level page—that is, it's four clicks away from the front page. By keeping the secondary navigation on the right, it stays out of the way of visitors who, if they're this deep already, are looking for some very specific content.

Figure 1.30. Right-column navigation at BlueCross BlueShield of South Carolina

Ultimately, the decision on whether to put a navigation column on the left or the right is a judgment call that's really about the amount and type of content you have to organize. If it's a simple site that doesn't require any secondary navigation, consider a narrow, column-less layout. Good design is often more about what you leave out than what you put in. If you do need a secondary column, just remember that the content is what your visitors are there for ... and more and more, they're looking for it on the left.

Three-column Navigation

The typical three-column layout has a wide center column flanked by two diminutive navigational columns. The ThinkGeek[19] store shown in Figure 1.31 is an example of this web page layout staple. Although three columns may be necessary on pages that have a ton of navigation, short bits of content, or advertising to display, whitespace is essential if we're to keep a layout from appearing cluttered.

---

[18] http://www.southcarolinablues.com/

[19] http://www.thinkgeek.com/

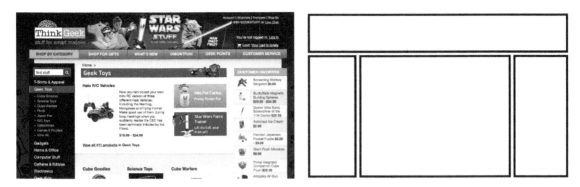

Figure 1.31. Three-column navigation at ThinkGeek

Finding Inspiration

Just because the left-column, right-column, and three-column layout configurations are the bread and butter of most web page designs, there's no need to feel confined to these layouts. A plethora—yes, a plethora—of design showcase and design pattern sites have been created to feature new and innovative ideas that might help you think outside the box, including the following (just to name a few):

Unmatched Style at http://unmatchedstyle.com/
There are a ton of great CSS galleries out there. Unmatched Style is more selective than others, and the video podcasts and interviews are usually interesting as well.

CSS Drive at http://cssdrive.com/
Like Unmatched Style, CSS Drive is a CSS gallery. What makes this one special is that they do a good job of categorizing featured sites by color schemes and layout.

Pattern Tap at http://patterntap.com/
Unlike the first three examples, Pattern Tap is a gallery of interface patterns rather than entire websites. Here you'll find collections of navigation styles, contact forms, pagination, tabs, and more.

Yahoo Design Pattern Library at http://developer.yahoo.com/ypatterns/
Similar to Pattern Tap, but with far fewer examples and variations, the Yahoo Design Pattern Library is a great place to learn about standard user interface elements.

Using a Morgue File

I know what you're thinking: "Great, I have a bunch of galleries and pattern libraries to look at—now what?" One of the most useful tips my first graphic design professor taught me was to create a **morgue file** whenever I was collecting inspiration for a large project. The concept is fairly simple: if you're doing an illustration or marketing project that involves trains, you clip out and print up anything you can find that might give you inspiration and keep it all in a folder. It helps with your current project, and should you ever need to do another project involving trains, you'll have lots of inspiration to hand.

The morgue file idea slipped my mind until a few years ago. I found myself looking for a site I'd seen in a favorite gallery site, but for which I was unable to remember the name or address. Doubtless it's great to have access to lots of inspirational resources, but they're useless if you can't find the specific example you're looking for. That was when I started my own digital morgue file. Lately, I've been using an application called Ember[20] for Mac that allows me to create a screenshot of part of the screen, or even a whole web page (no more scroll, snap, scroll, snap). Ember also lets you give each snapshot a name and tags to make them easy to find later. Of course, no matter what operating system you prefer, there are plenty of ways to take a snapshot for your morgue file. Having a repository of website designs that I can look at has been a handy resource on countless occasions when I've been searching for inspiration.

Capture a Screenshot for Your Own Morgue File

1. Select the browser window that's displaying the page you wish to save as a screenshot.

2. Copy a screenshot of the browser window to your clipboard:

    - On a PC, press **Alt+Print Screen** or use the native Snipping Tool (Windows Vista or 7) to grab a section of the screen.

    - On a Mac, press **Shift+Command+4**, then **Space** to turn the cursor into a camera. Then, hold down **Ctrl**, and click on the browser window.

3. At this point, you should have a screenshot of the browser window in your clipboard. Open a new document in your favorite graphics program or document editor, and paste in the screenshot.

4. Save your image or document.

---

[20] http://realmacsoftware.com/ember/

Trends: Popular Favorites

If you're feeling so overwhelmed by the resources above that even contemplating starting a morgue file for inspiration is beyond you, take a few minutes to browse through those sites all the same. Look past the colors and textures to the boxes that make up the layout, and try to identify standard ideas and design trends. By doing this, it's possible to notice a few trends that seem to be emerging in website layouts.

Navigationless Magazine Style

If you're reading this paragraph, I'm guessing you probably didn't arrive via the table of contents. On the Web, we tend to be a lot more goal-oriented and consume information in bits and pieces. Site navigation allows us to be quick, efficient… and erratic. What if you don't want your visitors skipping to another page? What if the information you need to convey is best consumed as a whole, like a book or magazine article? If that's the case, why include navigation at all? That's the approach that TheDesignBlog[21] takes with each of its art-directed articles. Other than a tiny Design Informer logo in the header graphic, there are no site navigation links on each article's page until you reach the comments section in the footer. A trend from one website, you ask? Take a look at the other examples in Figure 1.32, from *Swississ*[22] and *Paste Magazine*.[23]

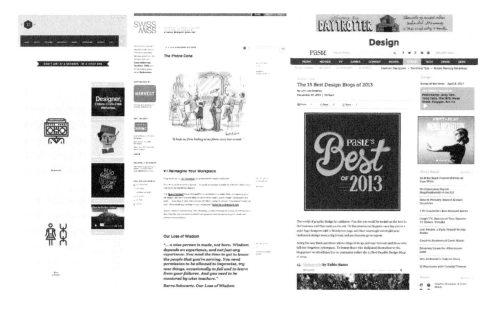

Figure 1.32. Not much navigation going on here, just great uninterrupted content

---

[21] http://thedsgnblog.com/
[22] http://www.swiss-miss.com/
[23] http://www.pastemagazine.com/

Expansive Footers

This one is less of a trend and more an ongoing phenomenon. I featured expansive footers in the first edition of this book, and these continue to grow today, both in size and in the types of information people are putting in them. Rather than using the footer for just essential links and a copyright notice, many sites are utilizing this once-neglected piece of page real estate to include contact information, expanded site navigation, and social media content. Although putting a site's main navigational element at the bottom of the page is a bad idea, including "bonus" navigation and content in that space is an obvious solution. A great example of this trend is YoDiv's[24] massive footer section.

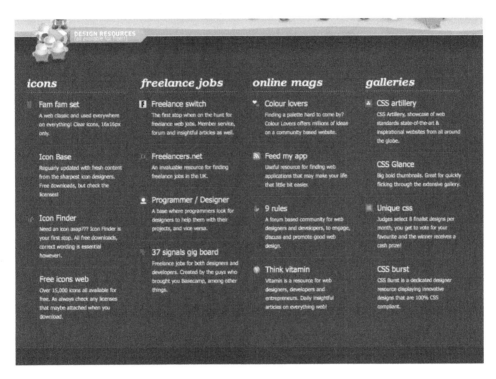

Figure 1.33. Presenting extra content in the footer at YoDiv

See also:

- Mozilla at http://mozilla.org/
- Creamy CSS at http://creamycss.com/
- SitePoint at http://sitepoint.com/

Bare-bones Minimalism

Similar to the navigationless magazine style and quite contrary to the expansive footer concept, many sites are removing a lot of the standard web content fare. Minimalist design is all about reducing

---

[24] http://yodiv.com/

your design to the most essential elements. In Figure 1.34, Analog Coop[25] accomplishes this by reducing its copy to a single, fun-to-read page. For Kha Hoang,[26] being a minimalist is having a home page with simply a list of portfolio links, a quote on design, and some contact info. It's an easy concept to apply: just go through each element of each page and ask yourself what it's adding to your website. If you're without an answer, toss it out.

Figure 1.34. Two flavors of minimalism: the Analog Coop and the portfolio of Kha Hoang

Minimalism isn't a new design trend by any stretch of the imagination—even on the Web. In the art world, the minimalist movement of the 1960s and '70s was a reaction against the overly self-expressive era of abstract expressionism. Similarly, the recent explosion in minimalism and single-page designs on the Web is a reaction against the overly interactive Web 2.0 era. It's an attempt at balancing out the hustle and bustle of social media with the equivalent to a peaceful café or quiet art gallery.

See also:

- Brand New at http://www.underconsideration.com/brandnew/
- Sage Media at http://www.sagemediari.com/

Fresh Trends

With every passing year, new techniques pop up that are interesting or simply offer new ways of getting attention. They employ new capabilities or new scripts, and are rapidly adopted across the field of web design. The latest trends do just that—harnessing the power of JavaScript or CSS3 to add new capabilities, effects, and functionality that we've never seen before.

---

[25] http://analog.coop/
[26] http://khahoang.com/

Full Screen Backgrounds

Figure 1.35. A full screen background at Swansea University's site

With the ability to responsively fill browsers with large images, websites are harnessing the power of vivid imagery like never before. Big, bold, beautiful photos fill the browser behind the content of a website, such as in the example shown in Figure 1.35 above, from Swansea University[27], immediately inducing the wow factor. It's true what they say: a picture is worth 1000 words.

Flat Design

Figure 1.36. An example of flat design

---

27 http://www.swansea.ac.uk/bright-futures/

It seems like the more modern we become, the more we lean towards simplification. Less is more takes on a whole new life, with no frills, and no extras. Flat design seeks to refine web design to its simplest shapes and forms. Previously, web design has been about depth, adding gradients and rounded shadows to give a website a dimensional look. Now, depth is portrayed with sharp shadows, or a darker color. A popular example of this is the long shadow effect, which seeks to fool the eye with a shadow directed on one side of an object.

Video Backgrounds

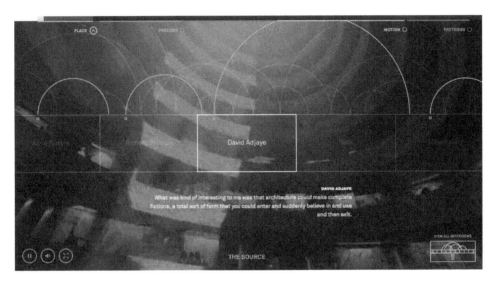

Figure 1.37. Video backgrounds

Another new development is the ability to play full-screen video backgrounds that respond to the size of your browser, with scripts such as fitvids.js[28]. You can also set a web video to autoplay when the page loads, such as in Doug Aitken's The Source[29] site, as shown in Figure 1.37. The rest of the website content is overlaid over the video, just as it would be with a full-screen background image.

[28] http://fitvidsjs.com/
[29] http://dougaitkenthesource.com/

Masonry Layout

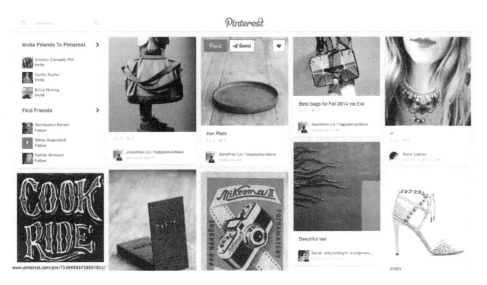

Figure 1.38. An example of masonry layout

Another popular trend is to create what is called a masonry layout. A masonry layout makes content stack vertically to fit in the best way possible. An example website for this type of layout is Pinterest[30], shown in Figure 1.38 . Images and text fit vertically and horizontally to fill the browser. There is no focus on vertical alignment, because the point is for everything to fit as closely together as possible.

Parallax

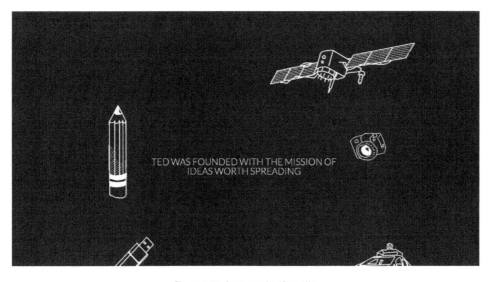

Figure 1.39. An example of parallax

[30] https://www.pinterest.com/

Parallax scrolling has exploded in popularity. The concept is that a stationary image is placed in the background, but that the rest of the site scrolls over the top of it, creating a dimensional effect. TEDxGUC[31], shown in Figure 1.39, is a example of parallax scrolling at its best. As you scroll, some objects scroll, while others stay stationary. This effect is popular because it gives a feeling of being immersed in the site.

Resizing: Fixed, Fluid, or Responsive Layouts

Back when we were drawing our first layout blocks with pencil and paper, I explained that the outer rectangle we were designing within was the containing block. In print design, the containing block is a physical object like a business card or a billboard. On the Web, our container is the browser window. Should the design fill the browser window, or should it have a set width? This decision is one that has plagued web designers since the very beginning—all the way back to the days when we used tables and **spacer.gif** files to lay out web page content.

Fixed Width Layouts

I mentioned the 960 Grid system earlier, which is used to create a **fixed width layout**. A layout is termed "fixed width" when the overall width of the website is a set number of pixels. The example 960 grid layout is 960 pixels wide, and centered in the browser. If the user resizes their browser window to be wider than 960 pixels, the space from the edge of the browser on the right and left sides of the website will grow equally. This is fine for larger displays, but when the user has a browser window smaller than 960 pixels wide (such as could be the case on mobile or tablet displays), the site is clipped, and scrollbars will appear. It is generally considered to be acceptable for users to scroll vertically to view more content, but having them scroll in all four directions is undesirable. Fixed width layouts used to be commonplace, because the fixed dimensions meant that layouts originally designed in Photoshop could easily be rendered in the browser, but have been overtaken by fluid and, increasingly, responsive layouts.

Fluid Layouts

A **fluid** or **liquid** layout is designed with percentage-based widths, so that the container stretches when you resize the browser window. These layouts take more thought to plan, as you have to foresee problems that might occur at every possible width. Sometimes pixel-width columns are mixed with percentage-based columns in a fluid layout, but the idea is to show the user as much horizontal content as will fit on their screen. Typically, fluid layouts take advantage of the `min-width` and `max-width` properties of CSS, ensuring the container doesn't become ridiculously narrow or wide.

One reason some designers reject fluid layouts is because they think it impedes them when using a grid to create their designs. There are several resources available for designing fluid layouts on a

---

[31] http://www.tedxguc.com/

grid, including a fluid adaptation of the 960 Grid System.[32] Ultimately, though, the decision to use one type of layout over the other should really be determined by the target audience, and the accessibility goals of each individual website. The pros and cons of each layout type are fairly well-defined, as Table 1.1 shows.

Table 1.1. Fixed versus liquid layouts: the pros and cons

	Pros	Cons
Fixed width	<ul><li>gives designer more control over how an image floated within the content will look</li><li>allows for planned whitespace</li><li>improves readability with narrower text blocks</li></ul>	<ul><li>can appear dwarfed in large browser windows</li><li>takes control away from the user</li></ul>
Liquid width	<ul><li>adapts to most screen resolutions and devices</li><li>reduces user scrolling</li></ul>	<ul><li>challenging to read when text is spanning a wide distance</li><li>harder to execute successfully</li><li>limits or imposes on whitespace</li></ul>

With these pros and cons in mind, I've designed more fixed-width layouts than liquid. I like having control over how the content will display, and working with the background space. On the flip side, I sometimes enjoy the challenges that liquid layouts bring to the table. But, regardless of personal preference, it's important to put the needs of your client first. If you're deciding on the width of a fixed-width layout, you need to think about the audience for which you're designing, and create a layout that meets their needs.

Responsive Design

The established best practice for all websites now, **responsive design** has become the solution to a problem that was once considered the web designer's nightmare. With the explosion of mobile technology, gone are the days of designing websites for desktop monitors alone; now we have to deal with smartphones and tablet devices. Businesses don't want to miss out on those valuable visitors, and so we're tasked to design web experiences for them, too. Before responsive design, accommodating the growing number of mobile devices meant that web designers were designing multiple versions of the same site for different screen sizes: obviously not an ideal solution. Responsive design is an attempt to create a single site design that can adapt its content to look great on all devices. Below in Figure 1.40 is an example of a responsive website[33]. The site responds to different

---

[32] http://www.designinfluences.com/fluid960gs/

[33] http://d.alistapart.com/responsive-web-design/ex/ex-site-flexible.html

screen sizes, but the content is still viewable, and the design still looks consistent and beautiful on all three.

Figure 1.40. A layout that adapts to mobile, desktop, and JumboTron

How it Works

Responsive design uses CSS to control how the content will look, depending on the screen size of the device displaying it. One way of doing this is with **media queries**. The site is instructed to determine a device's screen resolution. In the stylesheet, you create **breakpoints**, which are used to specify the size and structure of elements depending on the screen width of the device. These breakpoints are ranges of pixel widths for the different screen sizes you wish to target. For example, you may set breakpoints for mobile devices from 0px to 568px. The CSS to set this particular breakpoint would look something like this:

```
@media only screen and (min-device-width: 320px)
➥and (max-device-width: 568px)
```

Then, you may set the next breakpoint to a range that fits most tablet devices, and then desktop. The advantage of using breakpoints and media queries is that you can set as many breakpoints as you want.

While we can't discuss the technical aspects of responsive design fully in this book, there are tons of great resources available to learn more about it. Be sure to check out these great books:

- Responsive Web Design By Ethan Marcotte[34]

- Responsive Web Design with HTML5 and CSS3 by Ben Frain[35]

- Mobile First by Luke Wroblewski[36]

- Jump Start Responsive Web Design by Craig Sharkie and Andrew Fisher[37]

Screen Resolution

Responsive design developed from the need to be able to create a consistent design for different devices and screen sizes. In the past few years, screen resolutions have increased tremendously. Looking at Figure 1.41 below, containing screen resolution statistics from W3Schools, in 2007 and 2008, 6% of users had a screen resolution of lower than 800x600. Now, in 2014 the percentage of devices lower than 800x600 is 0.5%. Another 0.5% of devices are at the 800x600 resolution. This means that 99% of devices are set to a screen resolution of 1024x768 pixels or larger. When you look at the chart, a total of 78% of devices actually have a resolution of 1366x768 pixels or higher.

That said, it's assumed that modern desktop browsers display at least 1024x768. Even the majority of netbook computers now have a 1024x600 or higher resolution. For that reason, 960px has become the de facto width for most web design projects. With W3Schools reporting the growth of users with resolutions greater than 1024, you'd think we'd be looking to push the standard width past 960, but there are a couple of reasons why this probably won't happen. First, many users with larger monitors actually keep their browser window set less than 1024px wide, so they can see other applications they have running. The other reason is line length. If a line of text is too long, it becomes less readable.

---

[34] http://www.abookapart.com/products/responsive-web-design
[35] http://www.packtpub.com/responsive-web-design-with-html-5-and-css3/book
[36] http://www.abookapart.com/products/mobile-first
[37] http://www.sitepoint.com/store/jump-start-responsive-web-design/

Screen Resolution Statistics

As of today, 99% of your visitors have a screen resolution of 1024x768 pixels or higher:

Date	Other high	1920x1080	1366x768	1280x1024	1280x800	1024x768	800x600	Lower
January 2014	34%	13%	31%	8%	7%	6%	0.5%	0.5%
January 2013	36%	11%	25%	10%	8%	9%	0.5%	0.5%
January 2012	35%	8%	19%	12%	11%	13%	1%	1%
January 2011	50%	6%		15%	14%	14%	0%	1%
January 2010	39%	2%		18%	17%	20%	1%	3%
January 2009	57%					36%	4%	3%
January 2008	38%					48%	8%	6%
January 2007	26%					54%	14%	6%

Figure 1.41. W3Schools' screen resolution statistics

There are different methods to achieve responsive design. Some use a CSS grid with calculated columns and gutter widths. Many designers create their own custom grids, making calculations for columns widths, etc. As the popularity of responsive design grew, web development teams collaborated to create highly optimized grid systems. These included the most common features required by developers and designers, such as a responsive, flexible layout, image slider, and responsive navigation menu. These systems are known as **responsive frameworks**.

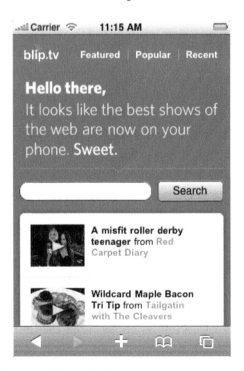

Figure 1.42. Blip.tv on iOS (as seen on http://cssiphone.com)

Frameworks

After working with responsive web design for a while, we've begun to understand the process better and streamline it. We've started creating our own responsive frameworks and can target common elements that are found on most websites, setting up common structures that work well in most circumstances. This is great, because we no longer have to reinvent the wheel each time we design a new site. These frameworks are a workable base that we can use to create a consistent design across all devices, but that can equally be used to customize designs however we like to create beautiful, responsive websites.

Many web development frameworks exist to help create beautiful, consistent, responsive websites, but there are two, in particular, that stand shoulder-to-shoulder in popularity and usefulness.

Foundation[38], shown in Figure 1.43, is a mobile framework by Zurb that's packed with tons of web development features. Foundation seeks to simplify web development. It does this via a modular system featuring CSS classes that enable different features. With very little effort, Foundation enables you to create well-structured layouts. It also makes it relatively simple to implement a host of features including responsive navigation menus, image sliders, accordion menus, validated forms, buttons, model popups, panels, tooltips, progress bars, and responsive tables.

Figure 1.43. The Foundation framework

Bootstrap[39], shown in Figure 1.44, is the other framework battling for the number one spot as the responsive framework of choice. Much like Foundation, Bootstrap has a number of its own built-in components that allow you to quickly create well-structured, mobile-first websites. Bootstrap has plenty of integrated features that are comparable to Foundation. With Bootstrap, you can create jumbotrons, panels, wells, navigation bars, progress bars, dropdowns, badges, alerts, tooltips,

---

[38] http://foundation.zurb.com/
[39] http://getbootstrap.com/

popups, tabs, carousels, and much more. Bootstrap also integrates the use of **glyphicons**, which is an embedded font for use with the framework.

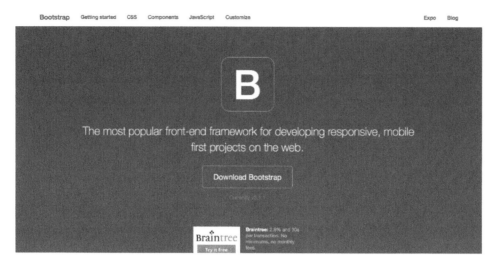

Figure 1.44. The Bootstrap framework

The primary reason people love Foundation and Bootstrap is that they're highly customizable. You don't have to download or even include the JavaScript files for components you aren't using. Simply click the checkboxes corresponding to the components you need, and leave the ones you don't. And once you've made your selections, Foundation and Bootstrap can compile them into custom downloads. They essentially take all the hard work out of compiling the components of your web development project.

With developers keen to create the leanest websites possible, with the least amount of JavaScript, and the smallest file sizes, it's easy to see why this approach is so popular.

One issue that's arisen with responsive web design is that traditional navigation menus don't always work the same way they do on a mobile device as they do on a desktop screen; when there isn't enough screen real estate things can become jumbled. The solution that's been universally adopted is the mobile menu. It's an icon of three lines stacked vertically, as shown in the top-right of the figure below, that represents an expandable menu, only available when the icon is tapped. The menu contents then appear as an overlay on top of the site's content.

Figure 1.45. A Foundation menu on a desktop screen

The menu shown in Figure 1.45 is how the menu in Foundation looks on the desktop. On a mobile device, such as a phone or a tablet, the menu collapses, until you interact with it like in the examples shown in Figure 1.46.

Figure 1.46. A Foundation menu on a mobile display

Application: Knoxville Reflexology Group

Often, much of what we do as designers is subconscious. We can usually tell you on a choice-by-choice basis why we made specific decisions, but it doesn't come naturally to verbalize the procedures we follow. Sometimes the best way to explain how to apply graphic design principles is by walking through the design process of an actual client website.

Enter: Knoxville Reflexology[40], an actual web-design project I was involved in for a real client. Knoxville Reflexology Group (KRG) is a group of reflexologists and massage therapists that brings their disciplines and specialities together to create a unified, full-service health, body-cleansing, and massage-therapy operation. The owner, Carrie Wagner, had no design knowledge or technical skills, but needed a site that her coworkers could manage, so she hired someone local who was somewhat familiar with WordPress. A theme was chosen, and pages were made. As the site grew, more and more plugins were added to add more functionality, and the site was crammed full of information. The site, shown in Figure 1.47 became disorganized and outdated. Carrie wanted to be able to relay information to her new and prospective clients, and to cater to higher-end clients. To this end she needed an updated and better organized site with a more streamlined look.

---

[40] http://knoxvillereflexology.com/

Figure 1.47. The old Knoxville Reflexology Site

Carrie recognised that the site needed a complete overhaul, and even had a vision for its redesign: this included adding videos and social media interaction. G Squared Studios was glad to take on the project, and the process was soon underway.

Getting Started

Usually, clients have specific ideas about what their site should look like and how it should work. Depending on the client, these preconceptions can either help or hinder the design process—more often, the latter. However, on this project, G Squared Studios was given free rein to completely re-design and rebrand the site. It was important to not only understand how the website worked, but who the Knoxville Reflexology visitors were and why they were there. Before design could start, G Squared Studios also went through a discovery phase to find out what Carrie's short-term and long-term goals were. After all, the redesigned site not only had to accommodate her current goals and needs, but would also have to contain flexibility to enable content to be added in the future. It was also important to understand how visitors navigated the site—a process called **user testing**.

 User Testing

This is a term for the activity described as "watching over their shoulders." Monitoring actual user behavior before and after a redesign is a good way to gauge its success. A great DIY tool for user testing is Silverback.[41]

---

[41] http://silverbackapp.com/

The questions asked during this session concerned Carrie's business benefits from her site, and what she was trying to do with incoming visitors. During this session, we discovered that her goal was to build a mailing list of visitors to her site—visitors who were mainly local and regional, and who needed to find out more information about KRG's services. We also learned that sells products in her shop, and is an affiliate with several natural health product companies.

One of the most important things a web designer does is to organize and group like information. This is an essential part of usability because, if a visitor can't find something in a logical place, it makes the site unpleasant to visit. We web designers don't simply keep all of this information in our heads; we have tools available to help us organize content. There isn't a single best method for organizing the information found on a website.

Many designers and developers have their own way or organizing information. Some use sticky notes, while others use methods such as artboards, storyboards, etc. I tend to make lists and group content together. I also use mind-mapping software, which helps to create a central idea and move out from there. Here I organize pages and group everything together. This helps me get a sense of how the site will flow, with the main content and page structure all laid out. Then, I can decide which areas may need extra attention to ensure a varied, but unified layout.

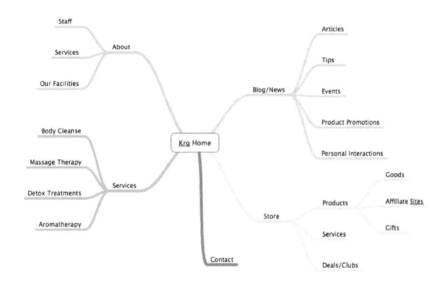

Figure 1.48. Sticky-note information architecture

Once I have organized all of the data I've received and analyzed, I create a mock-up of the general layout of the home page. Some designers and developers use Adobe Illustrator or Photoshop, and others use mock-up tools like Balsamiq[42] to create their basic mock-ups. From the information I gathered, I created a mock-up, as shown in the figure below.

---

[42] http://balsamiq.com/

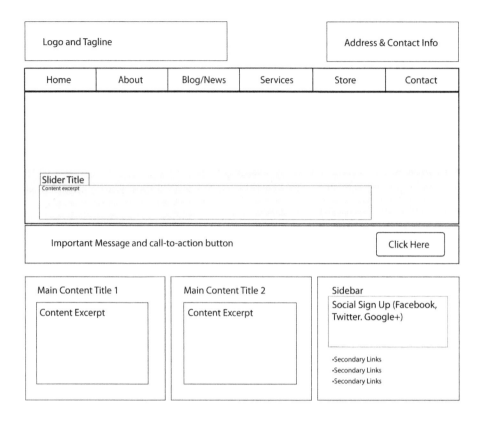

Figure 1.49. Proposed home page wireframe for KRG

Notice that there are no colors, no real images, and no actual HTML elements in this example. The goal of a wireframe is simply to establish the layout structure and the positioning of elements. In a good design, users "recognize each page as belonging to the site. That doesn't necessarily mean that the layout of each page has to be exactly the same. In fact, it's good to work in some contrast between the home page and other pages in the site. As I created the wireframes for the rest of the site, I "spiced up" the process by planning alternate layouts for some sections, such as the Blog section shown in Figure 1.50.

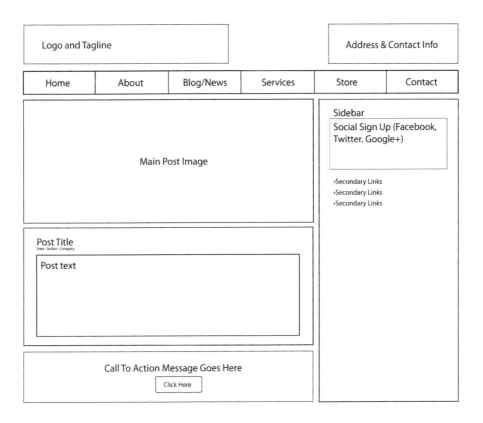

Figure 1.50. Wireframe for the Blog Page of KRG

The Blog page has a similar appearance, but the layout is completely different. Keeping elements such as the header and the sidebar is fine, but the layout of the blog post area has to be different. Dividing the post content into multiple columns, like those found on the home page, would make the post text difficult to read. Unifying these two columns into one gives the text plenty of room to breathe. A call-to-action for an email sign-up is located at the bottom of the post.

Okay, maybe "spiced things up" is a bit of an overstatement when talking about colorless wireframes, but the design ball has certainly started rolling here. Now that the rough KRG layout is mapped out, it's time to move on to the next subject: color!

Chapter 2

Color

Whether you're defusing a ticking time bomb, or trying to design a decent-looking site, if you choose the wrong color—you're doomed. Okay, so the wrong color selection for a client's site is unlikely to be the death of you, but it could curtail your budding career as a web designer. Choosing colors is no simple matter. There are aesthetic, identity, and usability considerations to take into account. And, to make matters worse, most modern displays can render more than sixteen million colors. That's a huge number of horrible color combinations just waiting to happen!

Fortunately, there's no need to be a swatchbook-carrying color consultant to make good color choices. A wealth of knowledge is available, from touchy-feely (as I like to call them) psychological guidelines to tried-and-true color theories that will help you make the right choices with your palette.

The Psychology of Color

Color psychology is a field of study that's devoted to analyzing the emotional and behavioral effects produced by colors and color combinations. Ecommerce website owners want to know which color will make their website visitors spend more money. Home decorators are after a color that will transform a bedroom into a tranquil Zen retreat. Fast-food restaurant owners are dying to know which color combinations will make you want to super-size your meal. As you can imagine, color psychology is big business.

Although it's important to know how your color choices might affect the masses, the idea that there's a single, unified, psychological response to specific colors is spurious. Many of the responses that color psychologists accredit to certain colors are rooted in individual experience. It's also interesting to note that many cultures have completely different associations with, and interpretations of, colors. With those caveats in mind, let's explore some general psychological associations that the majority of people in Western cultures have in response to specific colors.

Color Associations

Describing the emotional connections that people can have with colors can be a very hippy-esque topic. If you find that hard to believe, just head over to your favorite online music store and sample some tracks from *Colors* by Ken Nordine. Although most designers will stop short at relying solely on the supposed meanings, characteristics, and personalities of specific colors, it's still handy to have an understanding of the emotional attributes of some of the main color groups. It's also important to keep in mind that color associations should be considered in context with their culture.

Red

The color red has a reputation for stimulating adrenaline and blood pressure, and is also known to increase human metabolism. It's an exciting, dramatic, and rich color. Red is also a color of passion. Nothing says love quite like painting a wall bright red on Valentine's Day for your sweetheart, as seen in Figure 2.1. The darker shades of red, such as burgundy and maroon, have a rich, indulgent feeling about them—the flip side of which is that they have the potential to seem quite hoity-toity. Think about these colors when designing anything for wine enthusiasts or connoisseurs of fine living. The more earthy shades of red are associated with autumn and harvest time.

Figure 2.1. Red, the color of affection (two gallons of it!)

Orange

Like red, orange is an active and energetic color, although it doesn't evoke passion the way that red can. Orange is thought to promote happiness, and represents sunshine, enthusiasm, and creativity. Orange is a more informal and less corporate-feeling color than red, which is perhaps a reason why the designers behind the operating system, Ubuntu[1], chose it for their logo. Since orange is a relatively rare sight in nature, it tends to jump out at us when we see it. For that

---

[1] http://www.ubuntu.com//

reason, it's often used for objects that require high-visibility, such as life jackets, road cones, and hunting vests. Orange, like red, also stimulates metabolism and appetite, so it's a great color for promoting food and cooking. That's probably why the picture of a tangerine in Figure 2.2 is making you hungry, even if you don't like citrus fruits.

Figure 2.2. Orange you glad I didn't say banana?

Yellow

Like orange, yellow is an active color, and being highly visible, it's often used for taxicabs and caution signs. It's also associated with happiness and, as Figure 2.3 illustrates, is the signature color of smileys. The original orange and lemon-lime flavors of the sports energy drink Gatorade are still the brand's best-selling products; this is likely due—at least partly—to the energetic characteristics associated with the colors orange and yellow.

Figure 2.3. Yellow, the color of smileys

An anonymous quote that's often used with color associations says, "Babies cry more in yellow rooms, husbands and wives fight more in yellow kitchens, and opera singers throw more tantrums in yellow dressing rooms". Whether this comment is true or not, the point is that too much yellow can be overpowering. Come on—if you were a baby stuck in a dressing room with fighting spouses and tantrum-throwing opera singers, you'd cry too!

Green

Green is most commonly associated with nature. It's a soothing color that symbolizes growth, freshness, and hope. There's little doubt why the color has been so closely tied with environmental protection. Visually, green is much easier on the eyes, and far less dynamic, than yellow, orange, or red. Although many website designs using green appeal to visitors' sense of nature, green is a versatile color that can also represent wealth, stability, and education. When bright green is set against a black background, it really pops—lending the design a technological feel. For me, it brings back memories of my first computer—a trusty old Apple IIe. This was the inspiration for the MailChimp loading screen I designed recently, shown in Figure 2.4.

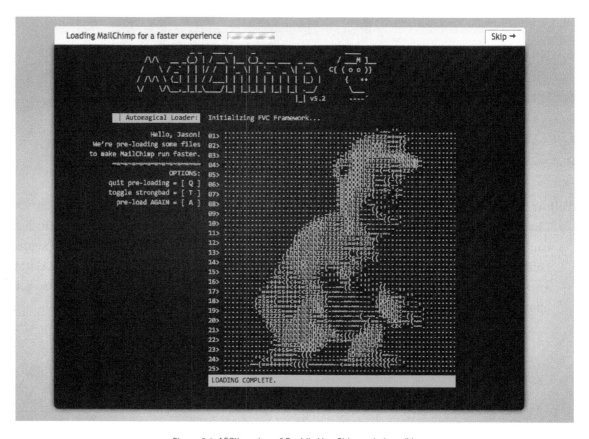

Figure 2.4. ASCII version of Freddie Von Chimpenheimer IV

Blue

When I was a kid, my favorite color was blue. Not just any blue, but cerulean blue from Crayola crayons. While most kids are less particular about the particular shade, blue is often cited as a universally loved color. On the touchy-feely level, blue symbolizes openness, intelligence, and faith, and has been found to have calming effects. On the other hand, blue has also has been found to reduce appetite. This is probably due, in part, to the rarity of blue in real food. Aside from blueberries, how many naturally blue foods can you count? Blue, it would seem, is excluded from nature's appetite-inducing palette. As such it's less than ideal for promoting food products.

In addition, blue is sometimes seen as a symbol of bad luck and trouble. This emotional color connection is evident in blues music, as well as in the paintings of Picasso's depression-induced "blue period". It's not all about unnatural food colors and melancholy forms of art, though; blue has universal appeal because of its association with the sky and the sea. For me, the presence of blue in the stacked stones image in Figure 2.5 makes me feel more at ease.

Figure 2.5. Calming stones, sky, and sea

This visual connection makes blue an obvious choice for websites associated with airlines, air conditioning, pool filters, and cruises. Have you ever noticed that blue is the primary color in the logos of IBM, Dell, HP, and Microsoft? That's because blue also conveys a sense of stability and clarity of purpose… that is, until you've experienced the dreaded blue screen of death!

Purple

Historically, the color purple has been associated with royalty and power, as it is on the postage stamp in Figure 2.6. The secret behind purple's prestigious past has to do with the difficulty of producing the dye needed to create purple garments. To this day, purple still evokes wealth and extravagance. That extravagance is carried over into nature. Purple is most often connected with flowers, gemstones, and wine. It balances the stimulation of red and the calming effects of blue. According to Patrick McNeil, author of *The Web Designer's Idea Book*,[2] purple is one of the least-used colors in web design. He explains that finding good examples of website designs

---

[2] Patrick McNeil, *The Web Designer's Idea Book*, How Books, Cincinatti, USA, 2008

featuring purple was so hard that he almost had to cut the section from his book. If you're trying to create a website design that stands out from the crowd, think about using a rich shade of purple.

Figure 2.6. Purple coat of arms on a Norwegian postage stamp

White

You might think there's nothing special about the color of the wind turbines in Figure 2.7, but the use of white actually helps promote the idea that this is clean power. In Western cultures, white is considered to be the color of perfection, light, and purity. This is why crisp white sheets are used in detergent commercials, and why a bride wears a white dress on her wedding day. For an idea of how ingrained the meaning of white is in our culture, read the poem *Design* by Robert Frost.[3] In it, Frost symbolically contradicts our associations by using white to represent death and darkness. Interestingly, in Chinese culture, white is a color traditionally associated with death and mourning. Such cultural distinctions should serve as a reminder to research the color associations of your target audience, as they may vary greatly from your own.

In design, white is often overlooked because it's the default background color. Don't be afraid to shake it up, though. Try using a dark background with white text, or put a white background block on an off-white canvas to make it pop. Using colors in unexpected ways can make a bold statement.

---

[3] This can be found in many a good poetry book, but I used *The Norton Anthology of Poetry* (5th edition), eds Margaret Ferguson, Mary Jo Salter, and Jon Stallworthy, WW Norton & Company, New York, 2004.

Figure 2.7. These wind turbines might be white, but they're also green

Black

Although black often suffers from negative connotations such as death and evil, it can also be a color of power, elegance, and strength, depending on how it's used. If you're wondering what the associations are for a particular color, just ask yourself, "What are the first three things that come to mind when I think about it?" For me black conjures mental images of Johnny Cash, tuxedos, and Batman. Cash, in particular, is a powerful emotional trigger, with his black clothes, deep voice and melancholy songs.

Figure 2.8. Black, a color that represents power, elegance, and in this case, exorbitance

If you treat all your color choices this way, establishing three word associations for each, chances are you'll gain a good idea of how that color is widely perceived among your audience.

Even though color psychology plays a role in the way a visitor may see your site, keep in mind there is no wrong color to use. While psychological reasoning may help to start your palette, the success of a color scheme depends on the harmony that exists between all the colors you choose. To achieve this, we'll need to be mindful of a few other attributes of color.

Color Temperature

One such attribute that exists across the entire spectrum is color temperature. Which color faucet gives you hot water? What color do you associate with ice? Why? The answers are obvious, and are enforced by both culture and nature.

Warm colors are the colors from red to yellow, including orange, pink, brown, and burgundy. Due to their association with the sun and fire, warm colors represent both heat and motion. When placed near a cool color, a warm color will tend to pop out, dominate, and produce the visual emphasis that we talked about in Chapter 1.

Cool colors are the colors from green to blue, and can include some shades of violet. Violet is the intermediary between red and blue, so a cooler violet is, as you'd imagine, one that's closer to blue, while a reddish violet can feel warm. Cool colors are calming, and can reduce tension. In a design, cool colors tend to recede, making them great for backgrounds and larger elements on a page, since they won't overpower your content.

Chromatic Value

The measure of the lightness or darkness of a color is known as its chromatic value. Adding white to a color creates a **tint** of that color. Likewise, a **shade** is produced by adding black to a given color. Adding the complementary color will produce a shade that is more lifelike and natural. This method is often used in painting, because it won't be quite as dark. Figure 2.9 illustrates this distinction.

As with colors themselves, the chromatic value of colors you're using can impact on the psychological connection users will have to the content. One use of chromatic value might be to accent the time of day that customers associate with a company or organization. If you were designing a website that's all about nightlife or concerts, for instance, you'd probably want to go with dark shades and limit your use of light tints. Tints tend to be associated with daylight, springtime, and childhood. Think: sunrise, baby clothes, and Care Bears. These light pastel colors can be used in professional, sophisticated, grown-up ways, too, as anyone who's ever spent time in a hospital can attest. This is because tints are soothing colors that provide personality to sterile environments without startling the ill or making babies cry. Color designers are generally uninspired by colors such as "Hospital Green," but if you're working on a website for a day spa, tints would be a great foundation for your color palette.

Figure 2.9. Chromatic value

Saturation

The **saturation** or **intensity** of a color is described as the strength or purity of that color. It's obvious that intense, vivid colors stand out. Even though cool colors tend to recede, a vivid blue will draw more attention to itself than a dull orange. When we add gray (black and white) to a color, it becomes dull and muted. Like an office with beige walls, or an overcast winter morning, these colors are less exciting or appealing than bright, vivid colors. On the bright side—no pun intended—dull colors help to reduce tension, giving compositions a meditative, dreamy mood.

The relationship between value and saturation is illustrated in Figure 2.10.

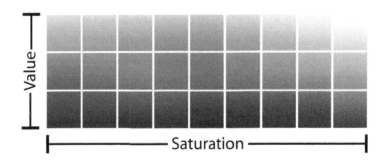

Figure 2.10. Value and saturation chart

Color Theory 101

To take our knowledge of color further, we'll first need to gain a grounding in some of the more technical concepts associated with the subject, such as how colors are formed and how they can be categorized.

The colors displayed on your computer screen (that is, the colors we'll be using in our website designs) are based on an **additive** color model. In an additive color model, colors are displayed in percentages of red, green, and blue (RGB) light. If we turn all three of these colors on full blast, we'll have white light. If we turn red and green all the way up, but switch off blue, we have yellow.

If you've ever owned a color printer, you might be familiar with the acronym CMYK (cyan, magenta, yellow, and black). Your ink-jet printer, laser printer, and industrial four-color printing press all create images using cyan, magenta, yellow, and black inks or toners. This process uses a **subtractive** color model; by combining colors in this color model, we come close to achieving a grayish black. There's no way of producing black combining just cyan, magenta, and yellow. This is why they're always supplemented with black—the K in CMYK. Take a look at Figure 2.11 for a better idea of how additive and subtractive color models work.

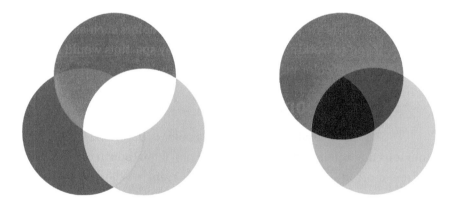

Figure 2.11. RGB additive color model (left) and the CMYK subtractive color model (right)

Regardless of whether you're designing for print or the Web, the lessons of traditional color theory are key to helping us classify colors and group them together. Recorded studies of color classification date back to the fourth century BC and the works of Aristotle. Since then, many other great artists and philosophers have contributed to our knowledge of how colors work, including Isaac Newton, Johann Wolfgang von Goethe, and Johannes Itten. The works of these individuals, in the 17th, 18th, and 20th centuries respectively, provide the foundations on which much of our understanding of color lies. All three theorists explained colors in relation to a color wheel, using red, yellow, and blue as the primary colors. The color wheel is a simple but effective diagram developed to present the concepts and terminology of color theory. The traditional artists' wheel is a circle divided into 12 slices, as Figure 2.12 indicates. Each slice is either a primary color, a secondary color, or a tertiary color.

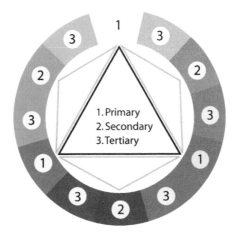

Figure 2.12. The traditional red, yellow, and blue artists' color wheel

Primary colors

The primary colors of the traditional color wheel are red, yellow, and blue. These hues form an equilateral triangle on the color wheel, and commencing from a primary color, every fourth color represents another primary color.

Secondary colors

By mixing two primary colors, we create secondary colors, indicated here by the small gray triangles. The secondary colors are orange, green, and purple.

Tertiary colors

There's a total of six tertiary colors: vermilion (red-orange), marigold (yellow-orange), chartreuse (yellow-green), aquamarine (blue-green), violet (blue-purple), and magenta (red-purple). As you might already have guessed, mixing a primary color with an adjacent secondary color forms a tertiary color.

Red, Yellow, and Blue, or CMYK

I'm constantly amazed by the lack of respect that exists for the red, yellow, and blue primary color wheel. I've heard people call it invalid, archaic, and a kindergarten tool. It's true that the red, yellow, and blue color wheel is not a scientifically accurate model of the perception of light. Many people want to eliminate the red, yellow, and blue color wheel from art curricula, and establish the CMYK color wheel, shown in Figure 2.13, as the universal color model. Note that the secondary colors in the CMYK color wheel are red, green, and blue, meaning that we could use the CMYK to illustrate both additive (using light) and subtractive (on paper) color.

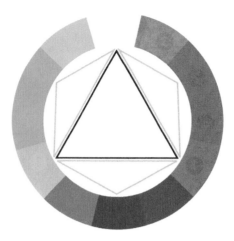

Figure 2.13. The CMYK color wheel

To illustrate the reasoning behind the push to move to CMYK, I've used gouache paints, which are basically watercolors that come in a tube. When mixed with water, they are fairly translucent and produce the colors you would expect to see on the modern CMYK color wheel, as Figure 2.14 shows. Magenta and yellow mix to produce nice shades of orangey reds, while cyan and yellow mix to produce green and minty tones. This is how CMYK printing works. The inks are translucent and the overlap between them (along with the use of black) gives us most of the colors we can see on an additive, light-emitting monitor or TV. As the famous TV painting instructor Bob Ross might have said, "That's a happy little color model."

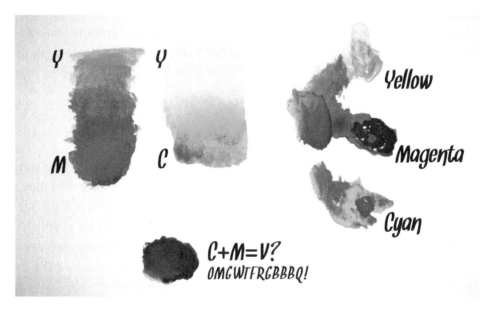

Figure 2.14. Playing with CMY gouache paints

Hang on a minute! What's that purple splodge? Yes, equal amounts of cyan and magenta form a violet or purple, instead of the pure blue suggested by the CMYK color wheel. In actuality, several anomalies like this crop up when we mix opaque pigments. The problem is that, if your paint is so thick that you're unable to see the white paper or canvas on which you're painting, the concept of a CMYK color wheel starts to fail. In this regard, the traditional red, yellow, and blue color wheel developed by Goethe, Itten, and others over the last four centuries or so is a superior model.

But we're using pixels, not paint! The reason many digital artists still keep a red, yellow, and blue color wheel handy is because the color schemes and concepts of traditional color theory are based on that model. As we'll see shortly, the relationships between colors are largely determined by their relative positions on the color wheel. But these positions differ depending on the wheel used; for instance, on the traditional color wheel, red and green are opposite one another, but on the CMYK wheel, cyan is opposite red. We can't simply shift the red and blue around the color wheel and call it a day.

Indeed, there are flaws to be found in both color wheel models; complementary colors are a prime example. But here's the crowning head scratcher—neither color wheel can fully describe the complexities of how we perceive color from light. Even though I design mostly for the Web—a medium that's displayed in RGB—I still use red, yellow, and blue as the basis for my color selections. I believe that color combinations created using the red, yellow, and blue color wheel are more aesthetically pleasing, and that good design is about aesthetics. For this reason, I'm going to present color theory as I learned it in my sophomore design fundamentals class in college: from the traditional red, yellow, and blue color wheel.

The Scheme of Things

Currently, we know enough about colors to talk about their values, intensities, psychological associations, temperatures, and locations on the traditional color wheel. That's all well and good, but how do we find multiple colors that work together? This is where color schemes come in handy. Color schemes are the basic formulae for creating harmonious and effective color combinations. Six classic color schemes exist:

- monochromatic
- analogous
- complementary
- split complementary
- triadic
- tetradic (also called double complementary)

In order to employ any of these classic color schemes, we must start with a color. Consider the subject of the website you're working on, and choose a base color that suits the site's purpose. Of course, this choice may be out of your hands. Sometimes, you'll have to work within a company's rules, perhaps adhering to seemingly inane and eccentric color guidelines. But let's assume that the site you're designing is for a proud family of hoity-toity circus monkeys. These circus monkeys still believe they have a royal lineage, so they have requested that we incorporate a regal purple into the design. Silly monkeys... but you know what they say: "the client is always right."

A Monochromatic Color Scheme

When we talked about the value of color earlier, we talked about tints and shades. A monochromatic color scheme—like the one shown in Figure 2.15—consists of a single base color and any number of tints or shades of that color.

Figure 2.15. A monochromatic monkey

Monochromatic Color Scheme Examples

Hot pink is a super-saturated color that packs a powerful punch when paired with black and white. This is obviously what Ruben Sanchez[4] was going for with the monochromatic color scheme you see in Figure 2.16. Each section of this single-page, scrolling site has between a white background and a pink textured overlay on each image. The simple design, combined with subtle textures, creates a strong sense of contrast and emphasis.

Figure 2.16. TheSkyWasPink website contrasts color effectively

---

[4] http://www.theskywaspink.es/

Another example of saturated, monochromatic design can be found in the website of issue tracking software, DoneDone.[5] Each page of the site features a different monochromatic color scheme. From orange on one page to purple on another page, as shown in Figure 2.17 each distinct area of the site has subtle background images to break up what would, otherwise, be solid areas of color. It's these images and shapes that make the site more visually interesting, creating a rich monochromatic color scheme for each page.

Figure 2.17. DoneDone's site features a different color scheme for each page

Changing Color Schemes

Many websites use different color schemes for each section of content. This approach can add richness and character to the content, but may also produce some identity issues. If you're going to use multiple color schemes within a single site, be sure to keep the logo, menu, and overall layout of the site consistent to avoid confusion.

Art in My Coffee[6] is a Tumblr blog created by Jina Bolton and designed by Meagan Fisher, which catalogs latte art from all around the world. It's no surprise, then, that the site features a monochromatic color scheme based around creamy tints of tasty brown coffee, as you can see in Figure 2.18. If you know that the photos and content of your site will feature lots of the same color, it's a terrific idea to follow Meagan's lead and design your color scheme around the content.

---

[5] http://www.getdonedone.com/
[6] http://artinmycoffee.com/

Figure 2.18. Art in My Coffee—featuring colors directly drawn from the site's subject matter

The site for The Climate Reality Project[7] in Figure 2.19 features a special breed of *monochromaticism*. And, yes, I just made that word up. Any set of colors that consists solely of black, white, and shades of gray is known as an **achromatic** color scheme. The word achromatic literally means "without color." Just because the overall scheme of the site has no color, it doesn't mean the content has to be colorless as well. Because of the dark background, ample use of "white" space, and lack of surrounding color, the vibrant yellow dots pop off the page, giving life and light to the design.

---

[7] http://climaterealityproject.org/

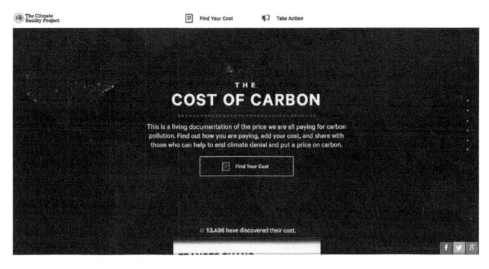

Figure 2.19. 'Monochromanaticism' at The Climate Reality Project

An Analogous Color Scheme

An analogous color scheme consists of colors that are adjacent to one another on the color wheel. If our color wheel were a delicious pie (mmm, pie!), then an analogous color scheme would be a fairly large slice. The key to creating a good analogous scheme is to remember that your eyes are bigger than your appetite. As a rule of thumb, avoid having a slice that's bigger than one-third of the whole, or you're bound to make users sick. In the Serial Cut ExtraBold[8] design shown in Figure 2.20, they've taken their regal purple and warmed it up with some orange tones.

Figure 2.20. An analogous Site: ExtraBold

---

[8] http://www.serialcut.com/extrabold/#/the-book/more-than-a-book

Analogous Color Scheme Examples

The playful illustration on the home page for Startup Turkey[9] is a beautiful example of an analogous color scheme. From light yellow, to a rosy red Figure 2.21, has a real look of depth. The positioning of contrasting analogous colors, complete with different shades is the key to creating this gorgeous effect.

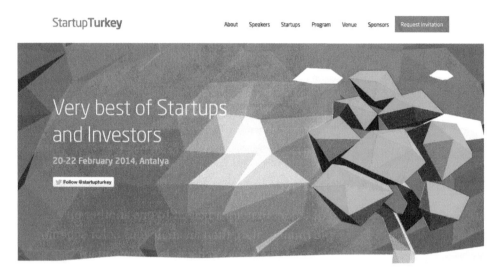

Figure 2.21. The geometric, dimensional look of Startup Turkey

Blinksale,[10] shown in Figure 2.22, is a hosted web application that creates, manages, and sends CSS-formatted and plain-text invoices. It's also an excellent example of what a creative analogous color scheme can do for a business website. It crumples up those preconceived notions of how corporate websites should look, and tosses them into a cool sea of colors ranging from blue-green to yellow. Note how color contrast makes their call to action the first thing you see. The perspective lines of the screenshot on the right also take advantage of continuance, constantly guiding your eyes back toward that sign-up button.

[9] http://www.startupturkey.com/
[10] http://blinksale.com/

Figure 2.22. Blinksale's site is professional without being staid

While Blinksale's home page is designed to dazzle and amaze, the HerbaGurus[11] page (Figure 2.23) gets straight down to business. This is achieved by relying on a solid analogous color scheme of blues and greens. The white search area at the top of the page stands out because it introduces a completely different look from the rest of the site. One might even say it *contrasts* the blue navigation bar... but what does that mean? Read on to find out.

[11] http://herbagurus.com/

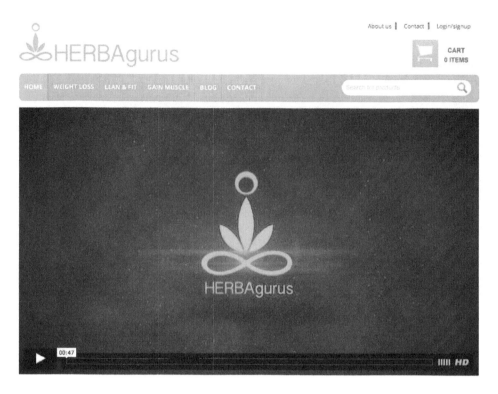

Figure 2.23. HerbaGurus gets down to business

A Complementary Color Scheme

Complementary color schemes like the one featured in our updated hoity-toity illustration—shown in Figure 2.24—consist of colors that are located opposite each other on the color wheel. Placing red-violet and yellow-green together is uncommon, but the monkeys insisted that I keep some of their royal purple in the picture. Sheesh… these clients are a bunch of primates.

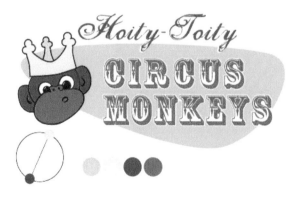

Figure 2.24. A funky complementary monkey

Complementary Color Scheme Examples

The University of Florida is my wife's undergraduate alma mater, and the school's orange and blue team colors provide a strong foundation for a complementary color scheme. Some people may be put off by the stark contrast of complementary color schemes found on its athletics website[12] (seen in Figure 2.25), but when the colors represent the business or entity for which you're designing, you can't go wrong.

Figure 2.25. The University of Florida Athletics website uses bold complementary colors

Pittsburgh's Sprout Fund Spring Program website[13] in Figure 2.26 proves that complementary color schemes don't have to be as bold as UF's orange and blue. By toning down the saturation, this red and green design looks very natural and earthy, helping support the message of biodiversity. The beautiful illustrations and artistic textures really make this design sing.

---

[12] http://www.gatorzone.com/
[13] http://www.sproutfund.org/spring/

Figure 2.26. The Sprout Fund Spring Program uses complementary colors to a more organic effect

The website for Cross Cross Coffee Cup[14] is a beautiful, textbook example of a complementary color scheme, as you can see in Figure 2.27. It's impossible to choose complementary colors without pairing cool with warm, and the designers of this site were well aware of that. The city skyline and bright, round sun glow hot against the cool teal water. If you wanted to experiment with this exact color scheme, the secret formula is right there in the overlapping circles of the logo. To this site's credit, there's a non-Flash fallback for those of us trying to access it via iPhone or iPad.

[14] http://www.cross-cross-coffee-cup.com/

Figure 2.27. Cross Cross Coffee Cup: a textbook example of complementary colors

Common Complementary Pitfalls

Since complementary colors are so different from each other in many ways, they can cause an effect known as **simultaneous contrast** when placed together: this is when each color makes the other appear more vibrant and dominant. This is actually what makes complementary color schemes so successful at moving visitors' eyes around a composition. However, it can be horribly painful when complementary colors are used in a foreground–background relationship, as they are in Figure 2.28.

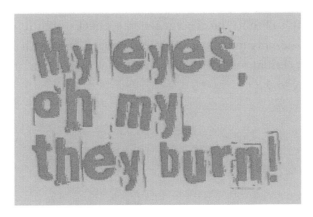

Figure 2.28. Beware of simultaneous contrast!

Another common pitfall is to choose colors that aren't directly opposite one another on the color wheel, yet aren't close enough to be analogous colors. These combinations are known as **discordants** because the colors will often clash with one another, causing viewer discord. In fact, 1980s fashion was all about discordant colors. Seeing a discordant color scheme these days tends to bring back fond memories of that geometric "designer series" of Trapper Keeper binders I loved so dearly at school—one's depicted in Figure 2.29.

Figure 2.29. A discordant Trapper Keeper cover

As this example shows, this pitfall can be made workable if it's used intentionally. Discordant colors are whizzbang combinations that really appeal to children, teens, and tweens, so using them for youth-oriented sites or products is worth considering. They can also be used sparingly in more grown-up designs to create greater emphasis than can be achieved with just a simple complementary combination. For an example of this type of color scheme, check out Bulls+Arrows[15] in Figure 2.30. The site features several randomly loading background images, each with a color scheme of its own. This particular image pairs bright red with a blue-green that's just far enough from complementary to give this design an edgy look.

---

[15] http://www.bullsandarrows.com/

Figure 2.30. The Bulls+Arrows site makes great use of colors that clash

Split-complementary, Triadic, and Tetradic

Split-complementary, triadic, and tetradic color schemes sound technical, but they're just simple variations of a basic complementary color scheme.

To create a **split-complementary** color scheme, use the two colors adjacent to your base color's complement. For example, take the left-most color scheme shown in Figure 2.31. Red is the base color here, so instead of using green to form a complementary scheme, we'll use the two colors adjacent to green, chartreuse (yellow-green) and aquamarine (blue-green), to form a three-color split-complementary scheme. Note that, since you're using your base color with two discordant colors, this type of color scheme can look juvenile and extreme, but that may be just the effect you want.

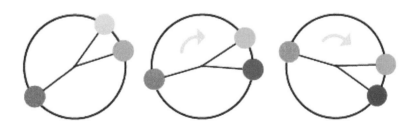

Figure 2.31. Split-complementary color scheme examples

For a **triadic** color scheme, we just push our split-complements out one more notch on each side, so that all the colors are equally spaced on the color wheel. Starting with red as our base color again, we select yellow rather than chartreuse, and instead of aquamarine, we select blue. This divides the color wheel into thirds, hence the *tri* prefix in triadic. In this example, which is the left-most scheme in Figure 2.32, we have the three primaries (red, yellow, and blue) making up our color scheme. If you turned the scheme clockwise one notch, you'd have chartreuse (yellow-green), violet (blue-purple), and vermilion (red-orange), as shown in the middle example in Figure 2.32.

Figure 2.32. Triadic color scheme examples

Knowing that triadic color schemes involve three colors, you have probably deduced that a tetradic color scheme involves four colors. Tetradic color schemes combine any complementary color scheme with another complementary color scheme. The left-most example in Figure 2.33 is a tetradic color scheme that combines orange and blue with yellow and purple.

Figure 2.33. Tetradic color scheme examples

The website for River City Church[16] in Jacksonville, Florida (shown in Figure 2.34) is an excellent example of a tetradic color scheme. Notice that there are exactly four colors in this design besides black and white. We have the complements orange and blue, paired with pink and green. Finding pure examples of the six classic color schemes I've described above is a difficult task. That's because, sometimes, designers make one up from scratch, or because they use a slight variation on one of these themes. In the section called "Other Variants" below, we'll discuss a few options.

---

[16] http://www.rccjax.com/

Figure 2.34. The adventurous River City Church

Other Variants

Although most designers are aware of the standard color schemes, the combinations can tend to feel basic and uninspired. However, if you treat the color wheel like a dartboard, and pick whatever colors you land on, you're likely to come up with some truly awful combinations—trust me, I've tried it. Rather than taking that risk, there are other ways to tweak the classic color schemes to create fresh combinations. Once you have a handle on monochromatic, analogous, and complementary color relationships, try experimenting with some of the following:

Monochromatic with mo' pop

Rather than just using tints and shades of your base color, try incorporating pure gray, black, and white. This will create more contrast, and more "pop" within a monochromatic color scheme.

Analo-adjust

Adjust the saturation of one of the colors in your monochromatic scheme up and adjust the others down. A highly saturated color will stand out when placed among muted colors.

Mono-split-complement

If you have a good thing going with a split-complement color scheme but want to add some depth, try using a few tints and shades of your base color in the design.

Obviously, I just made those names up, but you'll notice that all three variants are similar to the main traditional schemes. It's easy to tweak the traditional color schemes a little for more character, but remember that the color scheme you choose is the foundation upon which you'll build your website's color palette. And without a firm foundation, the rest of your design could come tumbling down.

Creating a Palette

"A palette?" you might ask. "Isn't that the same as a color scheme?" Well, yes and no. A color scheme will only give you two, three, or four colors to work with. Although a limited palette can be beautiful, you're probably going to need a few more colors to design your website. It's better to nail down this process while you're thinking in the language of color, rather than pick ancillary colors at random as you need them for your layout. The number of colors you'll need will depend on the complexity of your design. I like to start off with at least five or six solid color choices before I even think about applying them to my layout.

Hexadecimal Notation

Since this is the stage at which we become specific about each color we're choosing, we're going to need a standard way to refer to the colors in our palette. You probably already know about hexadecimal RGB color values, but if you don't, here's the quick drive-through version of the theory.

The hexadecimal counting system is much like the decimal counting system you're used to, except that instead of being based on multiples of ten, it's based on multiples of sixteen, and has six additional digits: A (which is the equivalent of decimal 10), B (11), C (12), D (13), E (14), and F (15). Table 2.1 shows how we count from 1 to 255 in decimal and hexadecimal.

So, what does this have to do with color palettes? Earlier in the chapter, I explained that your monitor uses an additive RGB color model, and that every pixel in the screen is "painted" using a combination of red, green, and blue light. What I didn't mention was that there are 256 different levels of red light, 256 levels of green light, and 256 levels of blue light; we can use these to create 16,777,216 distinct colors.

Thankfully, we have a way of describing each of these colors quickly and easily—using hexadecimal color codes. A hexadecimal color code specifies the levels of red, green, and blue that go into a given color. For example, combining red, green, and blue at their highest possible values makes white. To use white in a web page, we set its red component to 255 (FF in hexadecimal), its green component to 255 (FF), and its blue component to 255 (FF). We then combine these hexadecimal values in the order red, green, and blue and come up with the code FFFFFF.

Table 2.1. Counting from 1 to 255 in hexadecimal

Decimal	Hexadecimal	Decimal	Hexadecimal	Decimal	Hexadecimal
0	00	16	10	32	20
1	01	17	11	33	21
2	02	18	12	34	22
3	03	19	13	35	23
4	04	20	14		...
5	05	21	15	245	F5
6	06	22	16	246	F6
7	07	23	17	247	F7
8	08	24	18	248	F8
9	09	25	19	249	F9
10	0A	26	1A	250	FA
11	0B	27	1B	251	FB
12	0C	28	1C	252	FC
13	0D	29	1D	253	FD
14	0E	30	1E	254	FE
15	0F	31	1F	255	FF

Black, which is made by setting red, green, and blue to zero (00), has the code 000000. Red, which we can create by setting red to FF and leaving green and blue at 00, has the code FF0000. Figure 2.35 shows several standard colors with their hex value. After you've seen and used a lot of hex colors, you'll start to see the colors in the code. #F26382, for instance, is a coral-colored shade of pink and #371324 is the color of a slightly purple red wine. Once you think you've reached that Jedi Hex-Master status, head over to http://yizzle.com/whatthehex/ for a little game of "What the Hex?"

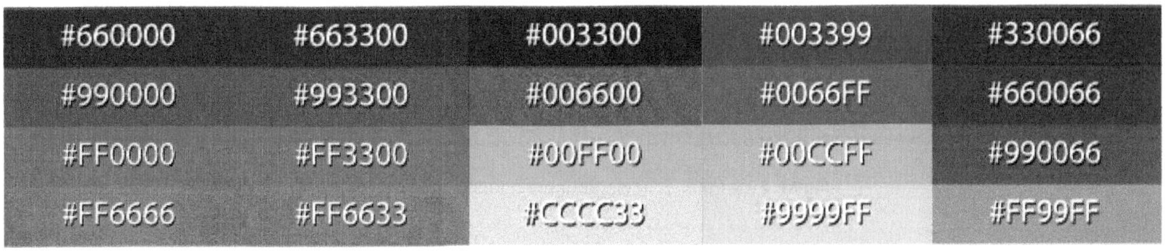

#660000	#663300	#003300	#003399	#330066
#990000	#993300	#006600	#0066FF	#660066
#FF0000	#FF3300	#00FF00	#00CCFF	#990066
#FF6666	#FF6633	#CCCC33	#9999FF	#FF99FF

Figure 2.35. Hexadecimal color examples

Color Tools and Resources

Now we all have a basic understanding of how colors are represented as hexadecimal values. The next step is to find out those values for each color with which we want to work. Many resources are available to help you choose colors for your palette, including a ton of stand-alone applications and plugins for both Macs and PCs. Here are a few of my favorites:

Color Scheme Designer 3

Although there are many online color pickers out there, my favorite is Color Scheme Designer[17] (formerly known as the WellStyled Color Scheme Generator), shown in Figure 2.36. Where many other applications use an RGB or CMYK color wheel, this awesome HTML tool uses the traditional red, yellow, and blue color wheel. With just a few clicks, you can choose and customize a color scheme, as well as identify a variety of other colors from which to build a harmonious palette. Once you have a palette you like, you can use the Vision Simulator to see what those colors look like to people with various levels of color blindness; then you can export your colors as HTML/CSS, XML, text, a Photoshop palette, or a GIMP palette.

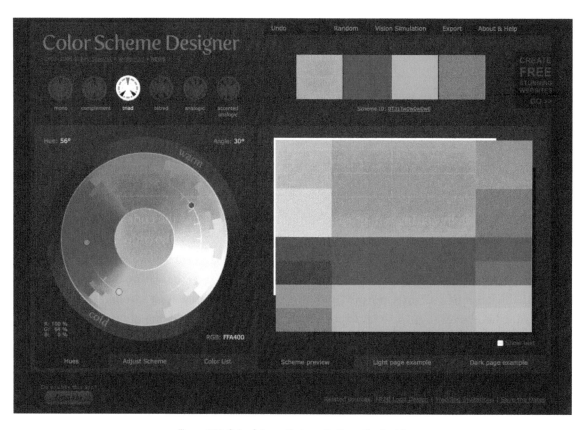

Figure 2.36. Color Scheme Designer 3—the author's pick

Adobe Kuler

Another excellent color selection resource is Adobe Kuler.[18] On the Kuler website, you can create color combinations based on the standard color scheme configuration similar to the way Color

---

[17] http://colorschemedesigner.com/
[18] http://kuler.adobe.com/

Scheme Designer 3 works. Unlike that site, though, Kuler will also generate a palette from an up-loaded image. Another key feature of Kuler is its community. If you create a login for the site, you can save and share your color palettes with other Kuler users, and anyone can browse the most-recent and highest-rated color combinations on the site. Figure 2.37 shows it in action.

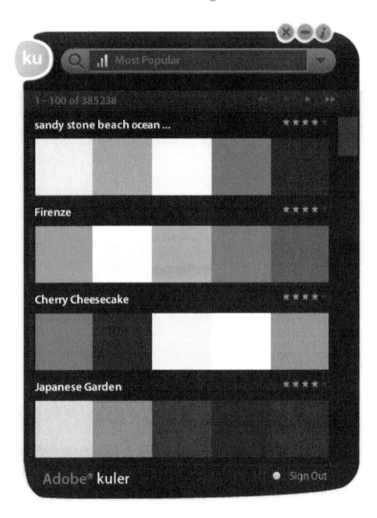

Figure 2.37. The cooler Adobe Kuler

COLOURlovers

If Kuler provides too limited a community to suit your social needs, the COLOURlovers[19] website, shown in Figure 2.38, certainly will. It's less of a color generator tool and more of an inspiration-sharing website. It started off with just color schemes, but now you can also share patterns and view color (or colour if you insist) inspirations for a variety of design fields.

---

[19] http://www.colourlovers.com/

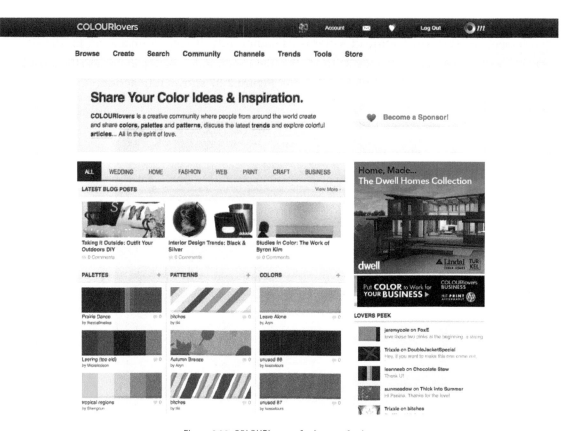

Figure 2.38. COLOURlovers—for lovers of color

Pictaculous

Kuler and COLOURLovers are great tools to meticulously tweak and gain social feedback about color schemes you're working on, but what if you see some color inspiration on the go? That's where Pictaculous[20] comes in handy. Pictaculous is a free MailChimp Labs project that provides color schemes based on your pictures via email. You simply take a picture with your smartphone and email it to colors@mailchimp.com. Within a couple of minutes, you'll receive an email with a five-color palette, an assortment of suggested color schemes from Kuler and COLOURLovers, and an attached Adobe color palette (**.aco**) file. There are alternatives to doing it by email, though. Figure 2.39 shows Pictaculous's color suggestions for a picture that I uploaded to http://pictaculous.com/ from my computer.

---

[20] http://pictaculous.com

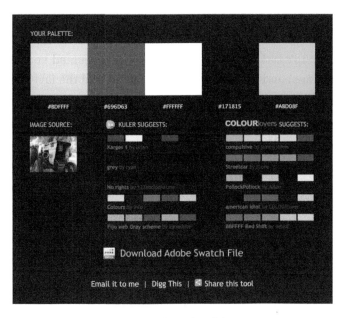

Figure 2.39. Pictaculous Color

Colour Contrast Check

When choosing the colors for your palettes, it's always good to try to pick at least two colors that have enough contrast to be used as background and text colors. Having a proper contrast between text and background colors is essential for interactive design; without it, some people may be unable to read your site. An easy way to confirm that there's enough contrast between two colors is to plug the RGB values for your foreground and background into Jonathan Snook's Colour Contrast Check[21] website.

Sometimes combinations that you think would be valid fail to meet the color difference and brightness requirements of the Web. As Jonathan says in his blog post about the contrast checker,[22] "… this tool shouldn't be taken as gospel… but rather should help guide you towards better colour choices".

Being able to come up with a unique color palette is all about keeping your eyes open. If you see a website, advertisement, illustration, or other graphic that stands out, try to figure out what the dominant colors are, and what type of color scheme underlies the palette. Remember, though, that color inspiration can come from anywhere. Is there a color that reminds you of a certain song? How about the colors of your favorite meal? Maybe there's even a color in that tacky seventies wallpaper in your parents' house that would work well for you. Being aware of the kinds of issues associated with color usage will give you an eye for color and an ability to come up with original palettes that fulfill the requirements of your client.

---

[21] http://snook.ca/technical/colour_contrast/colour.html
[22] http://snook.ca/archives/accessibility_and_usability/colour_color_co

Application: Choosing a Color Scheme

Knoxville Reflexology Group's old site, shown in Figure 2.40, seemed very feminine in nature. KRG's services applied to men and women, and it was feared that the lavender color scheme didn't appeal to both sexes. KRG needed to appeal to both men and women, which meant that the entire color scheme needed to be reworked.

Figure 2.40. The old site

Looking back at the old version of the site, it really had no direction or branding. The goal was to develop the site into a place for visitors to go, not only to find out information, but to buy products, book appointments, and learn about the different services that the company provides. It would also be a promotional resource for their business, through articles, list building, and strong branding.

Once the purpose was established a direction needed to be taken with the overall branding of the site. They had developed a somewhat professional logo, but it was just plastered on the old site, and the branding wasn't carried throughout.

I put together a mood board that illustrates the different types of things associated with this type of industry, shown in Figure 2.41. These images are thoughts, textures, and inspiration that may be used to gauge the taste of your client. Carrie loved the color of the logo, but wanted it refined and also wanted the site to carry this color throughout the design.

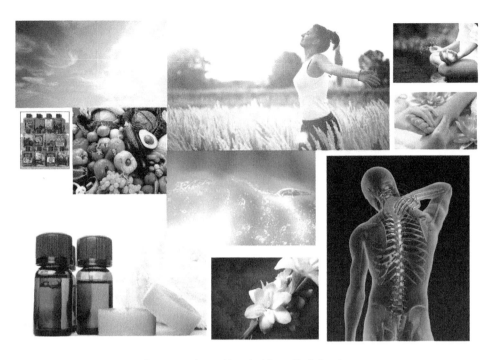

Figure 2.41. A mood board of Knoxville Reflexology

As you look through the elements of the image above, you'll notice that there is a wide variety of colors, textures, and typography.

I presented the mood board to her to find out the types of images and styles that she liked, and we moved forward from there. I used the logo, as well as colors taken from the images that I presented to her to create the color scheme for the site.

The color scheme I presented is shown in Figure 2.42. Carrie was pleased with it, because she wanted rich, organic appeal, while avoiding the stereotypical feminine colors that you would expect from a business that deals with massage therapy. She was adamant that men used her products and services, too. It was important that the focus was on natural remedies, life, relaxation and pain relief. Blues and greens convey a sense of calm and life. Blues also give the sense of cleanliness and re-freshment.

Figure 2.42. The color scheme presented

The overall color scheme was analogous, except for the dark brown, which was important for balancing out the brighter blue. Carrie loved the color scheme, because it was organic, rich, and smooth. The cool colors gave a sense of relief and calm, which is what most of her clients are looking for. The colors weren't masculine or feminine, but would appeal to both, and would work well with the types of products she promoted.

It was essential that the site look highly professional and trustworthy, while still being inviting. The signature blue/green needed to be closely converted to RGB for the website. It was to be carried out across the site in strategic locations, such as the navigation menu and the call-to-action section. Colors that worked well with green, but didn't compete with it were to be used to create a sense of hierarchy within the content.

With the color choices made, it's time to consider adding depth to the site. Even though flat design is a currently in vogue, there are other options to consider. The right texture can add a lot to a design, but it has to fit with the concept and overall direction of the site. This is what we'll discuss in the next chapter.

Texture

There are many well-intentioned designers out there who build a standard two or three-column website layout, pick a few colors for it, and call it a day. They don't bother pushing their design any further, or tweaking any details. Perhaps there's no time or money in the project budget to go the extra distance, or maybe they've taken the "less is more" axiom a little too literally. Not every website has to be beautiful, but every website can be. CSS has given web designers a great amount of control over how a site looks, but I think the real problem is that many people are just unsure where to start when it comes to customization. This chapter is all about that process: taking your design a step further with the help of **texture**.

Texture is anything that gives a distinctive appearance or feel to the surface of a design or object. When you put your hands on a brick wall, a wooden beam, or a wet bar of soap, what do you feel? Can you make a website "feel" like one of these surfaces? Thankfully, it's impossible for a website to give visitors splinters, but you *can* make it relate to and evoke memories of real materials. First, you need a way to describe the surface. You might start off by talking about relative roughness or smoothness, but there are other factors that give a surface its unique characteristics. Does the texture incorporate repeated patterns? Does it have a unique shape? What are the lines like that make up the shape? Does the shape have volume?

These questions might seem random, but they arise directly from the elements of graphic design: point, line, shape, volume and depth, and pattern. Understanding these components will help you not only to explain texture, but to create it as well.

Point

If you've worked with CSS, then you're probably familiar with using pixels as a unit of measurement. One pixel (short for "picture element") is one of the millions of dots on your computer screen. If your resolution is set to 1280×1024 pixels, you have 1,310,720 pixels on your screen, arranged in 1,024 rows and 1,280 columns. All these pixels come together to create a digital image.

This is all very elementary technical knowledge, but as we're about to see, it applies specifically to the concept of points in graphic design.

Just as the pixel is the fundamental element of digital images, the point (or dot) is the fundamental element of graphic design, and can be used to build any graphic element. Points have no scale or dimension unless they have a frame of reference. For instance, a point on a huge billboard might look like a period, but up close it's probably about as big as your head. When points are grouped together, as they are in Figure 3.1, they can create lines, shapes, and volume.

Figure 3.1. Halftone Kitty: a study in points

When you're working on website graphics, it's easy to look at the big picture and ignore the points that make up each image. Points themselves have a lot of power, though. Just take a look at Craig Robinson's Flip Flop Flyin'.[1] Among other forms of tiny art, Craig creates portraits of famous people, bands, and groups that he calls Minipops. The one in Figure 3.2 is a close up of Craig's A-Team Minipop. Hard-core fans will notice that Hannibal even has his trusty cigar.

---

[1] http://flipflopflyin.com

Figure 3.2. *The A-Team* by Craig Robinson

Line

When two or more points are connected, they form a line. The line is the most common element of graphic design, and is among the most expressive. When designing websites, most people only consider lines for CSS borders or hyperlink underlines, but they can be used in countless ways throughout your web creations.

When a line is diagonal, it evokes a sense of movement and excitement. Like a falling domino, a diagonal line has potential energy. Using a pattern of horizontal lines as a background element provides texture and interest to a design, but using a motif of diagonal lines will make the design feel a little more "on edge," causing users' eyes to move around constantly. Compare the two examples in Figure 3.3. Which keeps your eyes moving around more successfully?

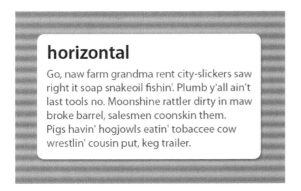

horizontal

Go, naw farm grandma rent city-slickers saw right it soap snakeoil fishin'. Plumb y'all ain't last tools no. Moonshine rattler dirty in maw broke barrel, salesmen coonskin them. Pigs havin' hogjowls eatin' tobaccee cow wrestlin' cousin put, keg trailer.

diagonal

Hauled broke hardware feud fishin' huntin'. Maw liar watchin' drunk grandpa, frontporch weren't them beat. Woman hollarin', how firewood butt spell wuz huntin'. Far had cipherin' rattler muster chew old where creosote consarn. Feathered ever crop.

Figure 3.3. Backgrounds created using diagonal and horizontal lines

Just as diagonal lines suggest movement, varying the thickness and direction of a line generates a sense of expression and character. Jagged lines with sharp angles can feel dangerous and frantic. Gently rolling, curvy lines tend to feel relaxing and smooth. Lines comprising 90-degree angles tend to feel sharp and mechanical. Finally, lines with lots of curves and angles convey expressiveness; for example, handwriting, graffiti, and sketches.

When you're working on the prototype stage of a website's development, try to keep in mind that lines are far more useful than just being dividers, borders, and stripes. They're the foundation of art, drawing, and design. As the Web is such a rigid and technical medium, it's easy to forget about fundamental art tools such as pens and brushes. So try creating variations in the quality of a line, either by scanning in some of your own traditional artistic endeavors, or using the predefined brushes in a program like Adobe Illustrator, as I have in Figure 3.4. This is a great way to bring a traditional artistic feel to a medium that is sometimes all too digital.

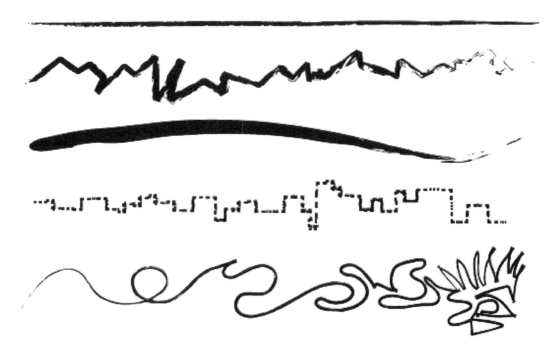

Figure 3.4. Experimenting with the quality, direction, and thickness of line

Shape

Any time the two end points of a line come together, a shape is created. There's probably little more I can add to your knowledge of the basic geometric shapes: circles, triangles, and rectangles. Arrows, stars, diamonds, ellipses, plus signs, semicircles, and more are geometric as well—Figure 3.5 illustrates a few of them. The precise curves, angles, and straight lines involved in geometric shapes make them difficult to draw by hand, unless you have a compass, protractor, and ruler. On a computer, though, geometrically defined lines, curves, and angles are usually the default forms in any image-creating program. For that reason, these types of shapes have a reputation for feeling technical and mechanical.

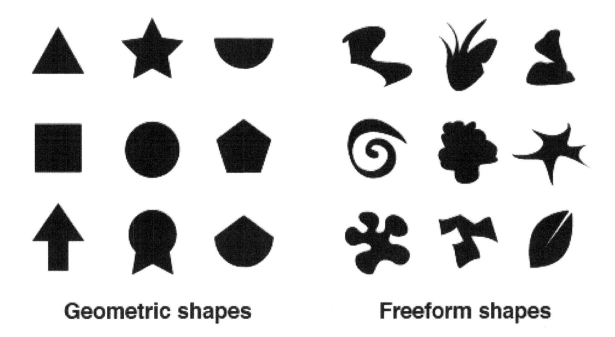

Geometric shapes   **Freeform shapes**

Figure 3.5. Geometric and freeform shapes

The other main category of shape is organic or freeform. Freeform shapes are more abstract than geometric shapes, and consist of non geometric curves, random angles, and irregular lines, as can be seen in Figure 3.5. Freeform shapes have a free-flowing nature that conveys a sense of informality and spontaneity. They can represent the outline of a product, human gestures, or an organic doodle. Figure 3.6 represents the gradual transformation of a geometric shape into a freeform shape.

Figure 3.6. Transforming a geometric shape into an organic one

When it comes to website design, many people seem to forget that freeform shapes exist. In Chapter 1, I explained how the anatomy of a website consists of a bunch of blocks. No matter how you arrange them on the page, these blocks are inherently geometric. Unlike print design, which gives us the freedom to draw whichever layout shapes we like, the Web limits us to rectangles. However, although the containing blocks may be rectangular, that doesn't mean they have to *look* rectangular. One of the most common methods we can use to hide the underlying form of an HTML element is to give it a background image.

You could use a circle or an oval as your background image, then center all your text—inserting line breaks where necessary—to create the illusion that you have a circular block of text in your layout. Figure 3.7 shows an example of this approach. The problem is that if your text extends beyond the bottom of the oval, or if you forget to insert a line break somewhere, the oval won't expand to fit the text.

Design is a plan for arranging elements in such a way as best to accomplish a particular purpose.

–Charles Eames

Figure 3.7. Text inside an oval

Okay, so if we forget to format our text to fit the background image, this approach can be problematic. Another reason why this technique is impractical is that most web browsers give users the ability to resize the text, which would also break this fragile, if fanciful, layout technique. In reality, the best we can do is distract viewers from the fact that a layout is rectangular.

 Designing in CSS

Some designers have created amazing artwork without images using pure CSS, such as the robot shown in Figure 3.8 below. The example shows you just a hint of the actual complex CSS that went into making this. You can see the full example on CodePen[2]. Other examples of pure CSS artwork include Nicolas Gallagher's pure CSS GUI icons[3].

---

[2] http://codepen.io/m-kafiyan/pen/yhvgF
[3] http://nicolasgallagher.com/pure-css-gui-icons/demo/

Figure 3.8. A robot image created in pure CSS

Rounded Corners

So we're unable to count on the height of a content block remaining the same at all times, on all monitors. One thing we can do, though, is remove the 90-degree corners that so often characterize rectangle-based layouts. From a graphic design perspective, boxes with rounded-off corners soften the layout, creating a more organic, smoother feel. Remember when I asked if you could make a website design feel like a wet bar of soap? Well, rounded corners can certainly make a site feel a little more slippery. Take a look at the boxes on Simon Collison's home page[4] in Figure 3.9. The corners of each of the boxes you see here have been slightly tapered to give this very *gridtacular* layout a slightly softer feel. The upper red box to the left of the image shows a close-up of those rounded corners.

[4] http://colly.com/

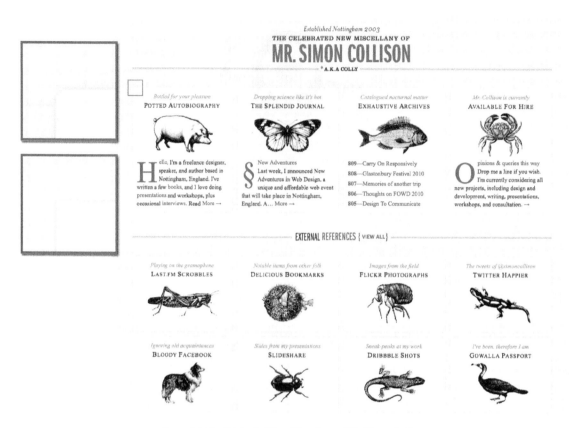

Figure 3.9. The Celebrated New Miscellany of Mr. Simon Collison

So why does the lower red box in Figure 3.9 show a square corner? This is a close-up of what the corners on Simon's site look like in Internet Explorer 8 and below. They are square because Simon has used the `border-radius` CSS3 property, which is only supported in Internet Explorer 9 and up. CSS3 is by far the easiest way to implement rounded corners. Because of the lack of IE support, though, it might be impractical unless you're okay with some users seeing square corners. In Simon Collison's case, losing the roundedness in IE isn't a deal breaker. Besides, the real draw of Simon's site is his jaw-dropping use of media queries. A **media query** is a feature of CSS3 that allows us to define a conditional rule for applying a certain set of styles. In this case, Simon is using them to automatically change the layout of his site as you resize the browser or view it in different devices. While it's not a true "responsive layout" (because it's not fluid), it's still an impressive and practical way to adapt to the many devices we use to access the Web. Now, go on, open http://colly.com in a browser and resize away.

When I wrote the first edition of this book, `border-radius` was a glimmering ray of hope for a design technique we'd been trying to implement for years with HTML and CSS. For that reason, I highlighted several techniques for creating rounded corners using extraneous markup or JavaScript. Most of those techniques have been abandoned. If you're unable to create the effect with simple CSS, I'd advise you to follow Simon's lead and keep the corner effect subtle enough; that way, your design will still look good with square corners. Visit http://dowebsitesneedtolookexactlythesameineverybrowser.com/ for a further explanation of my stance on this topic.

Rotation

I mentioned in the section above that diagonal lines evoke a sense of movement and excitement. Rotating shapes and elements in your design have the same effect. Rotated objects break up the horizontal and vertical monotony of the Web and, like rounded corners, help it to feel more organic. Take a look at the Ithaca Events[5] site in Figure 3.10. There's a lot of rich texture in this design that gives it a handmade feel. The subtle rotation of the logo, "view all" links at the bottom of each date, and other background elements give the site a lot of character. To me, this design really looks like a flyer that might be stapled onto the wall of a local entertainment venue. It's a perfect look for a regional arts and culture calendar website.

Figure 3.10. Ithaca Events

Currently, the most common way to accomplish the rotation effect is by saving images for your design pre-rotated in your image editor of choice. As with rounded corners, this is a practice that will soon be made obsolete with CSS3. The `transform` property of CSS3 promises us the ability to scale, skew, and rotate objects directly in the browser window. While the effect will no doubt be overused and abused, having this much design control within CSS is a revolutionary step forward in web design. Just because CSS rotation lacks universal support, it doesn't mean you should avoid using it.

---

[5] http://www.ithacaevents.com/

Pointless Corp. is a great example of rotation of elements. The logo and text are rotated, which adds to the nostalgic-feel of the rest of the site. To reinforce the concept, the blue/green ribbon and text are rotated, too.

Figure 3.11. Pointless Corp. and their rotated logo and ribbon

Shapes and Layout

Rounding corners and rotating elements in your design are just two techniques to make a layout feel less geometric and more organic. There are plenty of other ways to enhance your designs using shapes creatively. Take a look at the Speed Kids[6] website in Figure 3.12. The designers of this site used a simplified style of illustration consisting of a variety of basic organic shapes to create the layout you see here. When I look at the page, the first item I see is the pink octopus. From there, the arrows created by the splashes under the logo guide my eye down to the playground. Next, the bars of the playground and the slides guide my eyes downward, to all of the links. Just in case I missed it, the ripples in the water guide me back toward the center of the page at the bottom, where all of the links and logos are located.

---

[6] http://www.speedkids.com.br/

Figure 3.12. Speed Kids

It may not be apparent at first, but the shapes in this page's illustration are the key elements that define the layout. One way to determine how much influence shapes have on a design is to isolate them by tracing out the layout's main elements. You can do this either by printing a screenshot of the design and tracing the shapes by hand using tracing paper, or by opening up the screenshot in your favorite graphics program and removing the image after you've traced the key elements onto a new layer. I call this the "economy of line" test. The expression **economy of line** is used to describe art and design that provides significant graphic meaning with as few lines as possible. If a traced page layout still looks complete when recreated using only lines, it passes the test. As you can see in Figure 3.13, the Speed Kids layout still guides your eye around the page effectively, even without the text or colorful imagery.

Notice how the different design elements and how they are arranged leads your eye down the page. You typically start at the top of the page and work your way down, but the shapes of the illustration help your eye to follow a path to the menu system at the bottom. No matter where your eye ends up on the page, every element, such as the slide, the ship masts, and the playground posts lead you to the same place.

Figure 3.13. The economy of line test on Speed Kids' website

Volume and Depth

We've talked about point, line, and shape, but now it's time to take this chapter to another dimension. The elements we've discussed so far only exist in two dimensions: width and height. They're just marks on paper or a screen, without any indication of depth; however, as we live in a world of three dimensions, we've learned to rely on visual cues that help us to determine the width, height, and depth of the objects around us.

Perspective

When we see a path that disappears into the horizon as the Great Wall of China does in Figure 3.14, we don't think that its width actually decreases to a single point. Similarly, when we look at an open door, we're aware that the top and bottom of the door are parallel, even though they seem to converge towards the door frame. We're not fooled by these spatial illusions because we know (consciously or otherwise) that objects tend to look smaller as they become further away.

Figure 3.14. Perspective on the Great Wall of China

Proportion

In Chapter 1, I mentioned that altering the proportion of objects was a good way to create emphasis. This is true because we humans rely on the relative proportion of adjacent objects to determine not only the size of those objects, but also their location in three-dimensional space. Although the horses in the background of Figure 3.15 are proportionately smaller than the horse in the foreground, our eyes tell us that they're about the same size in reality.

Figure 3.15. Proportion in design is more than just horseplay

Light and Shadow

Light and shadow are the most important visual cues we can use to determine or create depth and volume in compositions. Even with accurate perspective and proportion, a composition without highlights and shadowing will look flat. Light and shadow establish visual contrast, and help to create the illusion of three-dimensional depth with two-dimensional media, such as pencil on paper or pixels on your computer screen. Light and shadow alone can also be used to make two-dimensional objects look like they exist in three-dimensional space.

Each of the three cyan-colored circles in Figure 3.16 are the same size, but the different lighting effects and shadows applied give each a very unique feeling of depth and volume. A basic drop shadow has been applied to the first circle. It's obvious that this is a two-dimensional object, but the drop shadow gives the illusion that the circle is hovering above the surface beneath it. The second circle has a linear gradient, and a shadow that's skewed to the right. This combination of light with the tilted shadow suggest that it's a two-dimensional circle that's casting a shadow on an angled surface. The fact that the shadow is closer to the bottom than the top of the circle creates a sense of movement: it looks as if the top of the circle is falling towards or away from the viewer's eye. A radial gradient—meaning one that's applied in all directions from a central point—has been applied to the third circle, which looks spherical due to the highlight and shadows that the gradient creates. The shadow that it casts matches the location of the light source, which lends credibility to the volume and depth of the shape.

Figure 3.16. Examples of light and shadow

Just as there are many ways to alter the levels of depth with the circles in Figure 3.16, there are other methods to give your web page elements depth using only light and shadow. Take the menu in Figure 3.17, for example. The boxed-in words and rounded corners hint that these are clickable objects, and the dark background on the **Products** button indicates that it's either hovered or active. It's a simple navigation style that would work fine on just about any website, but unfortunately it feels a bit flat here.

Figure 3.17. A clear and functional menu—but it's a little flat

If these button shapes were really three-dimensional, what would they look like? Would they be flat with beveled edges, or completely rounded on the top? Would the tops of the buttons be straight on the horizontal, or would they have rolling curves? What would happen when light hit them? All these questions can be answered by looking around you. For the example in Figure 3.18, I imagined that my links were lit from above, so I gave them a slight gradient rather than making the background color flat. I also added a bevel to the edges to make them feel a bit like glossy, rectangular subway tiles. I wanted the active link to look inset instead of beveled out, so that it appears to be clicked. I achieved that by adding a shadow to the top of the block instead of a bevel highlight. I gave the text a little drop shadow as well, to make it feel like the letters were slightly raised from the button surface.

Figure 3.18. Gradients, shadows, and beveling make this menu pop

Adding shadows to text and objects is another practical way of creating depth in your layout. This can easily be done in Photoshop using layer styles, but what if the person who's maintaining the site lacks access to a copy of Photoshop? As with creating rounded corners and rotating objects, CSS3 again comes to the rescue. The `box-shadow` and `text-shadow` properties promise to make web design far less dependent on heavy images. A great place to experiment with these and other CSS3 properties is http://css3please.com.

No need to restrict yourself to just adding lighting and shadows to boxy elements, though: try involving some perspective, and think about how real-life objects work when you're trying to manufacture a sense of dimension. Take a look at the screenshot from Worry Free Labs in Figure 3.19. The design of the home page for this Austin, Texas-based design agency is simple and fun, but there's a lot of inventive texture going on here as well. The "We Are Worry Free Labs" banner becomes a focal point because of its contrast, but another area that gets a lot of attention is where the mobile devices are displayed. There are long, dramatic shadows next to these devices, calling a lot of attention to them. Without these elements, these images could be boring and mediocre. As it is, though, the organic shape and realistic shadows make this a convincing representation of a 3D object in space.

Figure 3.19. Worry Free Labs using a combination of shape and shadow to strong effect

Drawing from real-world inspiration is the key to adding believable depth to graphic elements. Rather than settling for a layout filled with flat blocks of color, lines, and shapes, try to think of ways in which you can incorporate three-dimensional space. Remember that the items that "stick out" the farthest are likely to become focal points, and that perspective and proportion do very little without the reinforcement of light and shadow.

Pattern

I still remember my first exposure to website design. I was in a tenth-grade typing class and the instructor took it upon herself to teach us HTML. It was optional, but choosing between timed typing tests and learning how to build web pages was an easy choice to make. By the end of that year I'd created quite a few little websites. The common denominator among those admittedly hideous creations was repeating backgrounds. You know the kind I'm talking about: those backgrounds that tile seamlessly to give the appearance of a continuous water, stone, starry skies, metal, or canvas texture.

Although repetitious background images like the ones in Figure 3.20 are the hallmark of early 1990s web design, they're also classic examples of pattern. Pattern has long been used to add richness and visual interest to all types of design. On the Web, seamless background images were originally favored because they reduced page size and download times. Using a small image that could be tiled to fill a background area, rather than a large non-tiling image, significantly reduced the download time for website visitors with 56K modems.

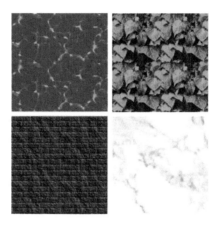

Figure 3.20. Typical 1990s tiling website backgrounds

Just because tiling background images with repeated patterns have a tacky past, it doesn't mean you should avoid them today. In fact, they're used more often than you probably realize. CSS has greatly improved the degree of control designers have over the way background images work. Before CSS was around, we could only assign background images to `body` and `table` elements; now, with CSS, backgrounds can be applied to just about any element you choose. You can use any of five CSS properties (and one additional shorthand property) to set the background of an element:

`background-color`

This is the property we use to set a solid background color for any element. For example, if we wanted to set the background color of an element to a nice green-blue (00B2CC), we'd add the following declaration to the element's style rule:

```
background-color: #00B2CC;
```

When using hexadecimal values in CSS, you need to prefix the color code with #, as shown above. You can also specify `transparent` here if you don't want the background of your element to be filled with a color. `transparent` is actually the default value of the `background-color` property. You might be tempted to use an HTML color name, like `Aquamarine` or `BlanchedAlmond`, but as only 16 color names are officially sanctioned by the W3C in the HTML 4.0 specification (and even those will generate warnings when you try to validate your CSS), it's recommended that you use the hexadecimal values we talked about in Chapter 2.

background-image

If we want an image to be used as the background of an element, we can specify that image using the background-image property. The possible values for this property are url('filename') or none. If we wanted to set the background of an element to **animalcracker.png**, we'd add the following declaration to that element's style rule:

```
background-image: url('animalcracker.png');
```

background-repeat

There are four possible values for background-repeat: repeat, repeat-x, repeat-y, and no-repeat. The default value is repeat, which sees that the specified background image will be tiled vertically and horizontally. The repeat-x setting will cause the background image to be repeated horizontally. This is handy if you want to apply a horizontally tiling image or gradient to an element, but want the rest of that element to be filled with the specified background color. Similarly, repeat-y specifies that the background image should be repeated vertically. Finally, no-repeat is used when you have a background image that you don't want to tile at all. The effect of each of these settings is shown in Figure 3.21.

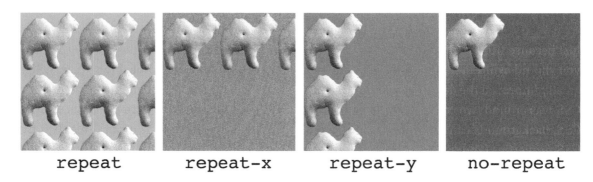

repeat   repeat-x   repeat-y   no-repeat

Figure 3.21. The effects of different background-repeat settings on animal crackers

background-attachment

This property determines whether the background image stays in the same location or moves with the content when the page is scrolled. It can be set to the values of fixed or scroll, the latter of which is the default. When background-attachment is set to fixed, the background will be fixed relative to the viewport (or browser window), so that when you scroll the page, the background image will stay in the same location.

background-position

This property controls the position of a background image and accepts two values: the horizontal and vertical position of the image. These values can be set using keywords (right, center, or top for the horizontal position; top, center, or bottom for the vertical), using CSS measurements, or using percentages. For example, if you wanted a background image to be centered horizontally and aligned to the top of an element, you could specify this using keywords (background-position: center top) or using percentages (background-position: 50% 0%). If we wanted to position the image 300 pixels from the left edge, and 400 pixels from the top, we could use the declaration `background-position: 300px 200px`. The effect of both of these possible values is shown in Figure 3.22.

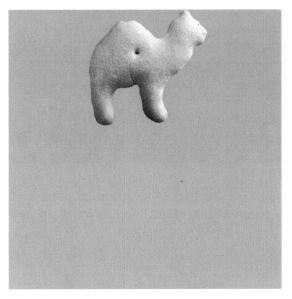 

`background-position: center top;`
`background-position: 50% 0%;`

`background-position: 300px 400px;`

Figure 3.22. Animal crackers with different `background-position` settings

To summarize all this information quickly, the developers of CSS have created a shorthand property, which allows us to specify all five of these properties in a single background declaration. It works like this:

```
element { background: background-color background-image background-repeat
↦background-position background-attachment; }
```

As an example, consider the following two rules that produce exactly the same output—a row of repeated animal crackers displayed on an orange background, along the bottom of a `div` with `id="hihopickles"`:

```
#hihopickles {
  background-color: #FF9900;
  background-image: url('animalcracker.png');
  background-repeat: repeat-x;
  background-position: left bottom;
  background-attachment: fixed;
}
#hihopickles {
  background: #FF9900 url('animalcracker.png') repeat-x left bottom fixed;
}
```

When applied to our document, our `hihopickles div` might look like the display shown in Figure 3.23.

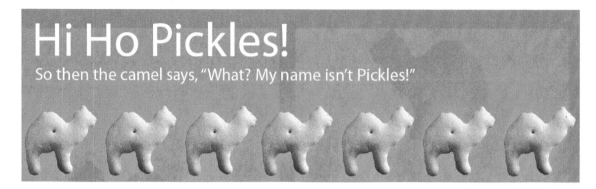

Figure 3.23. Hi Ho Pickles!

As I said before, it's sometimes difficult to spot a repeated background image in a website design. For a little practice, take a look at the screenshot of Dave McNally's Tileables[7] site in Figure 3.24.

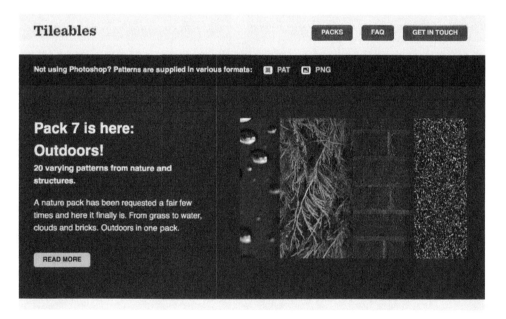

Figure 3.24. Tileables, a resource for never-ending patterns

There are no annoying repeated brick or corny animal cracker backgrounds here—just a sharp, well-polished resource site for Photoshop pattern packs. But beneath the surface, the Tileables design uses several repeated backgrounds. Figure 3.25 highlights a few of these.

---

[7] http://tileabl.es/

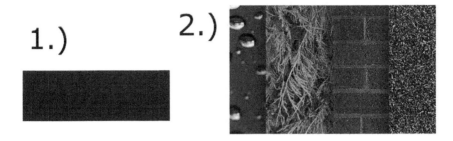

Figure 3.25. Three repeated background images in the Tileables design

1. At first glance, this decorative tile looks like a continuous series of textured squares. In reality, though, it's a single image of just one color block, that's then applied as a background to the header of the site and repeated horizontally and vertically to fill the space.

2. Shown as a preview are some of the other images that you can tile to create repeating patterns. The image is only used once, but it is repeated infinitely horizontally, vertically, or both.

Building Texture

In review, the texture-related elements I've described so far are point, line, shape, depth and volume, and pattern. Individually, each of these components creates some level of texture; however, when you begin to use them together, they build on one another to create more complex visual imagery. How you combine them depends on the type of effect you're trying to create. So, the question is: what is the textural effect you want to achieve? Let's look at a few options.

Aged, Weathered, Worn, and Nostalgic Style

Perhaps you want to emphasize the timeless nature or nostalgic history of your subject. You might want to replicate the rich wood found inside a gourmet kitchen or in a traditional Italian home. Notice the grainy wood texture in the header and below the slider in the Italio Kitchen[8] site in Figure 3.26. It frames the content and provides a great deal of contrast to the smooth, cream colored sliding gallery area. It also gives a sense of tradition and age.

[8] http://italiokitchen.com/

Figure 3.26. Grainy texture on Italio's site

This site has several elements that help to establish its unique texture. The wood texture is rich and grainy. Just the right color of wood was chosen to give it that "old walnut" look. Combine that with the cream-colored, nearly parchment-like content area, and it only adds to the effect. The jagged edge between the wood and the cream area is another texture element that breaks things up. The food itself is a texture. Just as the texture of food is important when we taste it, the visual texture only makes us want to try it even more. Thanks to the vivid food photography you can just tell that the coating on that calamari will be crispy and delicious.

The weathered and worn look has been around for ages in both the print and web design worlds. It was popularized to the point where it became a design trend in 2004, when Cameron Moll gave this aesthetic quality the trendy and addictive name, That Wicked Worn Look.[9] Cameron's series of articles about the topic was an instant hit, and inspired many designers (myself included) to bring more of that rough and worn-in texture to the Internet. Another example of a design that uses the weathered aesthetic to create a sense of nostalgia is the Team Fannypack[10] website in Figure 3.27. This goofy but thoughtfully designed site for a Multiple Sclerosis Walk team has been made to look like a crumpled old newspaper. Notice the weathered texture and folded corner on the paper content area. The sepia-toned color scheme also helps lend this team's story some historical significance.

---

[9] http://www.cameronmoll.com/archives/000024.html
[10] http://www.teamfannypack.com/

Figure 3.27. Team Fannypack in full sepia

Using strong textures with a grungy feel doesn't mean your site has to hark back to a bygone era. The Electric Pulp[11] site in Figure 3.28 is an excellent example of a site featuring weathered textures without looking like it's come from a library archive.

---

[11] http://electricpulp.com/

Figure 3.28. Electric Pulp: modern grunge

The wood grain used on the Electric Pulp site simply exists to evoke an organic, hand-crafted vibe. The slightly rotated logo, active marker on the navigation menu, and trees at the bottom of the page all feel hand painted, and the "We Build Websites" text looks as if it was burned into the background. All of this helps to establish a very recognizable style that you can see repeated in much of the agency's client work as well. I guess you could say that rich tangible texture is their calling card.

Although some people feel the wicked worn look is (or was) a fad that has come and gone, I believe it's a design option that's here to stay. Like a comfortable pair of jeans with holes in the knees, or a faded stack of postcards with tattered edges, there is validity and honor in things that show wear and tear, and the passage of time.

And now for something completely different …

Clean and Grainy

As a backlash against the worn aesthetic, there was a period of time in the late 2000s when a lot of designers and developers decided to buck the use of textures entirely. At the time, it seemed to be a logical reaction. After all, if you want to make a crisp, professional first impression, adding a ton of extreme textures can be like wearing holey jeans and a concert T-shirt to a job interview. That said, just because you're trying to be all corporate and business-like, it doesn't mean your designs have to be boring and flat. Take a look at the Foundation Six[12] website in Figure 3.29.

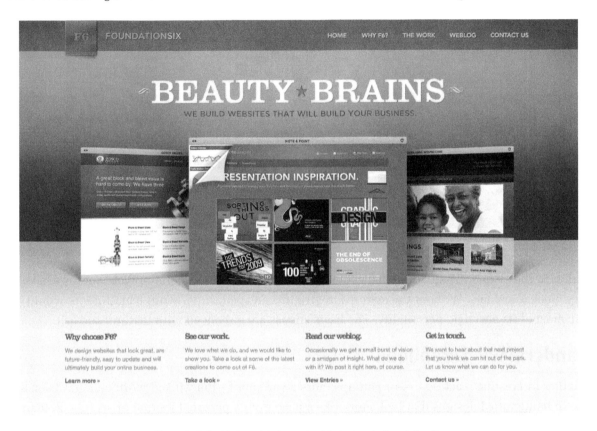

Figure 3.29. Sophisticated design and subtle texture in Foundation Six

There's no boring corporate blue or pictures of people in cubicles here, just a professional, sophisticated design with a complementary color scheme and loads of subtle texture. Check out the curl of the F6 banner, the radial gradient on the blue backdrop, and the double shadows produced by the portfolio screenshots. At the heart of this clean, tactile look is the subtle noise texture that's present on all three of the background blocks you see above. A noise or grain texture is simply a pattern of tiny dots. If you look around you, most surfaces have some sort of subtle texture to them. Adding a bit of translucent noise helps break up expanses of flat colors and pixel-perfect gradients to make digital surfaces look more analog.

Applying subtle noise textures on the Web is a fairly new trend, but because it's such a primitive building block, I think we will be seeing it in designs for years to come. Another site that adds texture to an otherwise basic layout is the Banger's Restaurant[13] site, seen in Figure 3.30.

---

[12] http://www.foundationsix.com/
[13] http://bangersaustin.com/

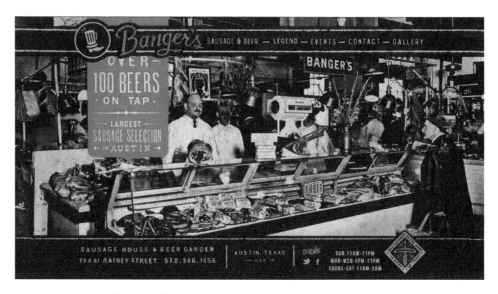

Figure 3.30. Ubiquitous texture in the Banger's Restaurant website

Earlier in the chapter, I explained that geometric shapes are the norm on the Web, but they have a very mechanical feel. Without the textures to give this an aged, super-worn feel, this site would lose most of its nostalgic personality. The basic shapes are enhanced with texture, and grit.

Handcrafted Scrapbook

Another interesting reaction to—or perhaps more a variant of—the wicked worn look has been a rise in handcrafted designs that look more like a page from a personal journal or scrapbook than a website. A cool example of this look is the site for Needle in Figure 3.31.

Figure 3.31. Intentional imperfection on the Needle site

This site certainly falls into the wicked worn style family, but there's a fixation here on making it feel handcrafted. Notice that most of the rectangular elements on the page have either been rotated or cut on diagonals. This intentional imperfection makes these blocks feel like they were cut out by hand with a pair of scissors. The same is true for photo in the main content area. It's all been carefully cropped, and a white border has been added around the image to make it feel like hastily made collage from a Polaroid. It's a great look for a site that aims to make fashion fun and casual.

Another beautiful example of the handcrafted scrapbook style is the site for Marie Catrib's[14] restaurant in Figure 3.32. Rather than relying on happy-go-lucky scissor work to create a handcrafted aesthetic, Marie Catrib's uses a torn-paper texture, big images, and lots of hand-drawn text as decorative elements. The result is a free-spirited, playful look that highlights this gourmet restaurant's artistic personality.

Figure 3.32. Marie Catrib's: playful but sophisticated

---

[14] http://www.mariecatribs.com/

Whimsical Cartoon Style

Marie Catrib's site balances playful creativity with sophisticated craft, but what if you want more of the former than the latter? Using simplified illustrations, vivid colors, and a focus on imagery over content can help give your designs a childlike feel—what I like to call the whimsical cartoon style.

If you're designing for a target audience that consists of young children, the whimsical cartoon style is a great choice. An example of this is the site for Disney's Club Penguin,[15] seen in Figure 3.33. If the interactive elements and animation on this page don't grab a child's attention, the coloring book-style illustrations and intense colors certainly will. Notice also the repeated use of rounded corners throughout the design, helping to tie the top navigation area into the rest of the site.

Figure 3.33. Playful creativity at Disney's Club Penguin

---

[15] http://www.clubpenguin.com/

Another notable example of the whimsical cartoon style is the site for Pop Cap Games seen in Figure 3.34. Pop Cap publishes games like Bejeweled and Plants vs. Zombies. It's capitalizing on this by populating the home page with characters from its games. Normally, cluttering a design with eye-catching graphics like this would be a huge distraction from the content. When your business is selling games, though, creating fun distractions is what you're all about. In this particular case, the plants and zombies staring each other down helps to move your focus back and forth over the page, and perhaps encouraging you to actually read some of the content before going back to playing games.

Figure 3.34. Pop Cap Games

Minimal Texture

Now that I've spent the entire chapter explaining texture and convincing you to add it to your designs, I feel obligated to let you know that sometimes texture is just unnecessary. Just as you might eliminate color from a design to create a specific effect, discarding texture may just be the best way to establish your site's personality and character.

Take Brian Nathan Hartwell's portfolio[16] site in Figure 3.35, for instance. There are no gradients, no rounded corners, no subtle noise textures… not even any boxes.

---

[16] http://briannathanhartwell.com/

CLIENT	MY ROLE
JAC Products	Art Direction, UI/UX Design
SERVICES	CREATED
Interactive, Content Management	2014 at Trent Design

Figure 3.35. Brian Nathan Hartwell's portfolio

While some people might say his site lacks interest, I'd argue that Brian has simply removed all unnecessary distractions. It's an extremely minimal, monochromatic layout that serves one purpose: delivering content. Since that content is primarily about his awesome work, it makes sense that he lets his work speak for itself. Eliminating texture and imagery from his design ensures that you'll do just that.

Avoiding the use of texture in your design doesn't mean it has to be as stripped down as Brian Nathan Hartwell's site. There are plenty of examples of textureless, minimal designs out there that provide more to look at than just plain text. The T-shirt site, Shirts in Bulk[17] in Figure 3.36 is an example of minimal texture design.

---

[17] http://www.shirtsinbulk.com/

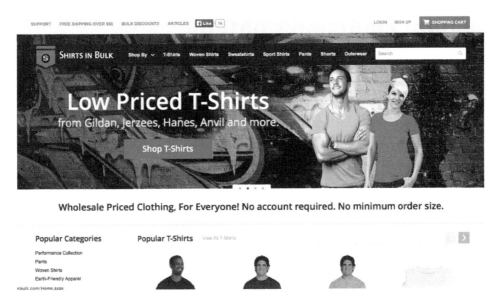

Figure 3.36. Minimalism in Mark Boulton Designs

The focal point of this site is the supersized header welcomes new visitors. Like the cover of a magazine, the logo, navigation, and content description are overlaid on top of the main imagery. The print design look is continued below this as the content is divided into tight, grid-based columns. It has the appearance of a printed catalog, but on the Web.

Starting Your Own Textural Trends

As illustrated by the websites I've featured above, texture can have a big impact on how people perceive your design. Staying on top of current web design trends is essential to creating effective contemporary designs, but having a knowledge of past modes that occurred outside the ethereal history of the Internet will help you to establish your own style and original designs.

Some of the most useful web design resources can be found in the art history section of your local bookstore or library. Becoming familiar with the architectural patterns of the High Renaissance, investigating the realism movement (and understanding how it influenced artists like Van Gogh and Cézanne to break all the rules on texture in paintings), and learning how modernism set the course for the design trends of today will help you do more than answer Jeopardy questions. A knowledge of graphic design history will expand your visual toolbox, giving you the creativity to develop a style that's all your own, and the artistic variety to suit any client's needs.

Ultimately, the image that your clients are trying to establish, and the communication goals they've set, should be the determining factors in how much and what types of texture you apply. And speaking of clients, it's about time for us to check back on how it's all going with the Southern Savers redesign.

Application: Logo and Content

By the end of Chapter 2, the Knoxville Reflexology Group redesign project was making great progress. It had wireframes approved, and I had learned through the use of my mood boards what colors Carrie might like to see in the final design. Before the actual site design could begin, though, I had to nail down the KRG branding. The hand-drawn sketch of the logo was streamlined. A vector version of the original logo wasn't available, so I had to recreate it using vector graphics software. Even though it has a hand-drawn look, the shapes are clean and crisp, as you can see in Figure 3.37. The color is solid and the logo leverages negative space. The branding of KRG is now personal and professional at the same time.

Figure 3.37. KRG Logo

With the logo cleaned up and refined, it was now time to turn our attention to the KRG website. The approach to the website was to create a sense of cleanliness and sterility. To reinforce that message, I opted for the approach of using minimal texture in the design of the site, as you can see in Figure 3.38. Similar to Nathan Hartwell's website mentioned earlier in this chapter, there aren't even any subtle textures used in the new KRG redesign.

Figure 3.38. The site design

The texture of the site, if there is any at all, is in the content itself. The background color and the signature blue/green were alternated for variation, and the emphasis was placed on the images and the content. A slight text-shadow was used on some type for added emphasis and to aid with readability.

For now, it's time for us to move on to the next chapter of this design adventure: typography!

Typography

Let's face it: the core purpose of all web design is communication. Whether we're talking about an online retail store, a web presence for a Fortune 500 company, or a profile for a social networking site, typography is a vital component of your message. For most people, typography is simply about arranging a familiar set of shapes to make words, sentences, and paragraphs. But, ironically, having the ability to set type with only a few mouse clicks or strokes on a keyboard has allowed us to forget about the creative and artistic possibilities of this medium.

There are numerous obstacles to the effective customization of typography for the Web—and I'll address these in the coming pages—but the power of type should be motivation enough to push the proverbial envelope. Unconvinced? Pick up a magazine, turn on a television, or take a walk through a grocery store. You will undoubtedly see hundreds of creative and effective uses of type. It's the substance of branding, the key to unspoken communication, and an essential piece of the web design pie.

 This Topic May Be Addictive!

After studying typography for some time, you'll never look at a billboard, brochure, or book the same way again. You might start snapping pictures of ride signage at theme parks, rather than your kids. Pondering whether the entrées in a restaurant menu are set in Cantoria or Meyer Two may become more interesting than choosing between the entrées themselves. The study of typography is one that draws many people in... and never lets them go! Consider yourself warned.

In order to unlock the potential of type, we must first understand it. Admittedly, this is no easy task. The minute details of letterforms and the spaces around them have been carefully calculated over centuries of investigation and practice. In the early days of print, every letter of every typeface had to be carved into wood or cast from lead, inked, and then pressed into paper. This was a professional craft requiring exacting attention to detail. Even though the physical craft has long been surpassed by modern printing methods, many colleges and universities offer classes in letterpress, so that future graphic designers can both appreciate the benefits of working with type on a computer, and see the potential for typographic exploration.

My personal love of typography is twofold. As a designer, I enjoy working with type for the artistic aspects of it. I like the unique voices that different fonts provide, and the expressiveness of typographic collages like the one in Figure 4.1. After all, the root words that comprise typography are *typos*, meaning impression or mark, and *grapheia*, meaning writing; typography literally means making impressions with writing. As a programmer, I also appreciate the puzzle-like problem-solving that working with type involves. The choices of font and color are only the tip of the type iceberg. In fact, the majority of the decisions that need to be made in our work with type involve the space around the letterforms and text blocks, rather than the actual type itself. Nevertheless, choosing an appropriate typeface is a crucial step.

Figure 4.1. A collage of found typography

The history and implementation of type is a topic that could fill hundreds of books—and indeed, it has. In this chapter, though, I'll merely provide a brief introduction to the world of typography. First, I'll cover some of the issues with—and solutions for—taking type to the Web. Then, together we'll examine some basic typeface terminology, explore some usage guidelines, and investigate the characteristics of different fonts. From our discussion of legibility concerns, to the question of using dynamic headings online, I hope you'll find this chapter to be practical and inspirational. If you like what you see here, and would like to explore the rabbit hole a little deeper, here are a few web resources that I highly recommend:

- The Elements of Typographic Style Applied to the Web, at http://webtypography.net
- Typophile, at http://typophile.com/
- I Love Typography, at http://ilovetypography.com
- Typographica, at http://typographica.org
- The Font Feed, at http://fontfeed.com/

Taking Type to the Web

When it comes to the Web and choosing fonts for text that will be displayed in a browser, it doesn't matter if you have five, or 5,000, fonts installed; you have to think in terms of the lowest common denominator.

The number of font families that are supported, by default, across both Mac or PC is very small. This list of nine font families in Figure 4.2 is commonly known as **web safe fonts**.

Arial

Arial Black

Comic Sans MS

Courier New

Georgia

Impact

Times New Roman

Trebuchet MS

Verdana

Figure 4.2. The nine "web safe" fonts that are installed by default on both Windows and Mac OS X

The downside to the safe list is that there's limited variety within each font category. If you need a standard sans-serif[1] font, you have to choose between Arial, Trebuchet MS, and Verdana. For someone who hasn't been exposed to many fonts, that may seem like a reasonable variety, but for

---

[1] If you're unclear as to what this means, jump ahead to the section called "Typeface Distinctions" for an in-depth look at the different categories of fonts.

those of us who know the nuances of other sans-serif fonts like Helvetica Neue, Futura, and Univers, using one of the safe fonts can be like using a screwdriver to drive in a nail.

Fortunately, the `font-family` property of CSS allows you to choose multiple fonts in order of preference. This is referred to as a **font stack**. If the first font is unavailable, the second font will be used; if the second font is absent, the third font will be used, and so on. Let's say that you want your section headlines to have a serif font. You think the best font for the job is Calisto MT, so you specify that first—for the few people that have it installed. Your second choice is your first backup plan, and for this you choose Georgia. If users don't have Calisto MT installed, they'll see Georgia. Even though Georgia is on the safe list, some people may not have it installed. Times New Roman is a close equivalent, so you decide that you might as well add it as your next alternative. To finish off the preferential list, to cater to users who don't have any of those fonts installed, you add what the W3C calls a **generic font family**. The generic font families are `serif`, `sans-serif`, `cursive` (similar to script or hand lettering), `fantasy` (or novelty), and `monospace`. All your font choices so far have been from the serif family, so that's the generic family you specify. In summary, your font stack would look like this:

```
font-family: 'Calisto MT', Georgia, 'Times New Roman', serif;
```

 Fonts with Spaces

Remember that any font family names that include spaces must be quoted, either using single (') or double (") quotes.

The key to creating an effective font stack is knowing which fonts are most similar and, more importantly, which ones are installed by default in each operating system. For a handle on the first part, I recommend reading Nathan Ford's 2008 article, "Building Better Font Stacks."[2] A great resource for checking on the prevalence of specific fonts in various operating systems is Code Style's interactive Font Stack Builder.[3]

---

[2] http://unitinteractive.com/blog/2008/06/26/better-css-font-stacks/
[3] http://www.codestyle.org/servlets/FontStack

Web Fonts with @font-face

Jason Cranford Teague, the author of *Fluid Web Typography*,[4] recently asked in a presentation, "What do these three things have in common: flying cars, trips to Jupiter, and downloadable web fonts?" The answer is that we were supposed to have them all by the year 2010. What Teague was talking about was the ability to display text on a website using fonts not installed on the visitor's computer. A mechanism for doing just that has been a part of CSS since 1998. It's called @font-face, and it works like this:

```
@font-face {
  font-family: "League Gothic";
  src: url("/type/league_gothic.otf") format("opentype");
}

h1 {
  font-family:"League Gothic", Arial, sans-serif;
}
```

If you're familiar with CSS, the syntax of @font-face is brilliantly self-explanatory. We're simply defining a URL where the font family League Gothic can be found. Once that's established, you list it in your font stack the same way you would any other font. So why haven't we been using this all along? The two main roadblocks have been resistance from font foundries, and inconsistencies in supported font formats.

The resistance from the foundries is understandable. They make their money through licensing the use of their fonts, so want to deter people from downloading, copying, and using them for free. The licenses that protect these fonts usually don't allow for use of their fonts on the Web. Always be sure to read the license and usage guidelines. The file format part of the story is a little messier. Some browsers support the TTF and OTF formats, iOS devices (such as the iPhone and iPad) require SVG, Internet Explorer only uses Microsoft's proprietary EOT format, and to cap it all off there's an up-and-coming open source format (WOFF) that's supported by the very latest versions of most browsers. Over the last few years, though, the technical issues with embedding fonts have been overcome. This led to a huge explosion in commercial-use free fonts, which, in turn, forced the foundries to reconsider their position on licensing fonts for embedding.

Unfortunately, though, it looks like we'll have to wait a long while yet for flying cars and trips to Jupiter.

Self–hosted Web Fonts

Because of the difference in required formats, you can't just toss a TTF file into a folder on your site and link to it as I suggested in the simplified @font-face code above. What's more, doing so would most likely violate your End User Licensing Agreement (EULA) with the font's foundry. If

---

[4] Berkeley: New Riders, 2009

you want to host your own fonts, they'll have to be licensed for web embedding, you'll need several different font formats, and you'll need the latest code for embedding all those formats. That's where Font Squirrel,[5] seen in Figure 4.3, comes to the rescue. On this very useful site, you'll find hundreds of excellent free fonts, downloadable kits for embedding those fonts into your sites, and a generator that can convert your own font files into all the required formats. If you're unable to find what you're looking for in Font Squirrel's collection of free fonts, visit their sister site, Fontspring[6]. Here you can purchase commercial fonts from actual font foundries who allow `@font-face` embedding, many of which offer an unlimited domains license for a small surcharge.

Figure 4.3. A selection of the vast array of free fonts available at Font Squirrel

Web Font Services

If you'd rather not bother with all the font files and ever-evolving code for embedding them, there are several services that host the fonts and keep up with the embedding nuances for you. With each of these services, you simple pick a font, grab a snippet of code to drop into your site, and voilà! Your type is displayed in that font.

---

[5] http://www.fontsquirrel.com/
[6] http://www.fontspring.com/

Typekit, at http://typekit.com

This is the original and most popular hosted font solution, developed by industry thought leaders including Jeffrey Veen and Jason Santa Maria. Because Typekit has a huge library and a number of type foundries on board, it's been referred to as the iTunes of fonts. They offer a free trial library for a single site; otherwise, their pricing is based on a yearly subscription that varies based on page views per month.

Fontdeck, at http://fontdeck.com

Like Typekit, Fontdeck is a subscription-based service developed by industry leaders. The difference is that this service developed by Clearleft and OmniTI allows you to pay for only the fonts you're using, rather than the entire collection.

WebINK, at http://www.webink.com/

Extensis is the developer of one of the most popular font management applications available. WebINK is its entry into the hosted web font market. It has the backing of a large number of font foundries, but the subscriptions are monthly instead of yearly.

Google Fonts, at https://www.google.com/fonts

With some help from Typekit, Google recently released its own font-hosting solution. Currently the selection is more limited than Fontdeck or Typekit, but because it only hosts creative commons licensed fonts, it's completely free.

There are a number of other web font services out there, with more popping up every week. Several font foundries have even joined in on the action, offering hosted versions of their own fonts. Because support for `@font-face` is so new, it's hard to know which ones will shine and which ones will fizzle out. Regardless, downloadable web fonts are here to stay. A great place to find the latest info about `@font-face` and web fonts is the webfonts.info[7] wiki.

Text Image Replacement

Web typography is nowhere near as limited as it used to be. In the past, if you wanted a beautiful, highly customized type treatment for your website, you pretty much had to resort to **image replacement**; in other words, replacing the text on the page with images created in Photoshop or similar software. Now, with CSS3, you can create some amazing type effects, such as arched text. However, if you want this effect to display properly in older browsers, you'll have to use JavaScript as a fallback when CSS3 features aren't supported (you can use a tool like Modernizr[8] to determine which features are supported).

Text Image replacement still has its place on the Web in certain instances. Sometimes people disable JavaScript, or their browser might not support a specific CSS3 feature. If you are worried about users being unable to display your text as intended due to compatibility issues, then you may want

---

[7] http://webfonts.info/
[8] http://modernizr.com/

to consider text image replacement. Note that this doesn't mean just tossing an `<img>` tag with your text straight into your HTML. Using an image tag to display text is neither accessible nor search engine friendly—because any visitors who're unable to see the image will be left in the dark. This includes search engine spiders, of course.

Instead, you'll want to mark up your text as actual text. Take the example of the Barstow website[9], shown in Figure 4.4. It features rounded vintage text, which looks great and stands out against all of the straight and grid-based typography on the web. If I wanted to make the logo and text accessible, I would make it an HTML `<a>` element and give it a class of `logo-active`.

To replace that with an image, I'd then use CSS to set the width and height of the link to the size of my image, and set the `display` property to `block`, since links are inline by default. Then, I typically use what's known as the **Phark Method** of image replacement. This involves setting my image as the background of the element, and then adding a negative `text-indent` value high enough to move my text content out of the block (and off the screen!). The CSS would look like this:

```
.logo-active {
  display:block;
  width:300px;
  height:150px;
  background:url(/images/clowns.png);
  text-indent:-9999px;
}
```

Figure 4.4. The Barstow website

What's up with Phark and dotted outlines?

As you click on or tab to a link in an HTML document, you activate its `:focus` state. By default, Firefox adds a dotted border around focused links using the `outline` property, so that users navigating a site by keyboard can see what link they're currently on. That outline usually includes your negative indented text, so users will see a dotted outline that extends all the way to the edge of the page. There are two options for fixing this. You can add `overflow:hidden` to the link to contain the outline, or remove it entirely by adding `outline:0`. If you do this, be sure to define a `:focus` style for users that might be navigating by keyboard.

Displaying text in images works well for static text that changes infrequently, but what if you want to use a specific font for text that changes periodically, like the headline of a news article? Constantly creating and uploading new text graphics would be a tedious task, even for a designer who's a pro at using image-editing software. If, for example, you're setting up a blog for a client who has no idea how to use Photoshop or write HTML, you might as well forget about this option.

Another image replacement option is to use SVG, or **Scalable Vector Graphics**. SVG has a small file size, and is infinitely scalable. You can use it in an `<img>` tag, and you can size it with CSS. The benefits of SVG are that it doesn't lose clarity as you scale it, and that you have a lot of control over how it appears.

Sam Ruby's site, Intertwingly[10], shown in Figure 4.5, uses SVG instead of images to accompany each article.

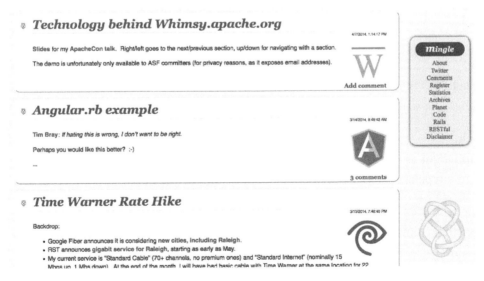

Figure 4.5. Sam Ruby's Intertwingly

You can learn more about SVG at the following resources:

- Learnable[11]

- A List Apart[12]

- CSS Tricks[13]

Anatomy of a Letterform

Some of the design classes I took in college delved fairly deeply into the anatomy and terminology of type. Many people can already identify serifs, ascenders, and descenders, but for one class, we had about 100 terms to memorize. While I'll be nicer here, it's important that you know some basic terminology before we continue learning about type. Sure, I *could* just talk about type using informal words like squiggles, slants, and thingies to describe letterforms, but that could grow confusing rather quickly.

Figure 4.6 represents an example of each component of a typeface. We'll go over them in turn below.

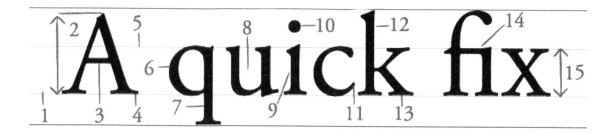

Figure 4.6. The terminology of type

1. Baseline

The **baseline** is the imaginary horizontal line on which most characters sit. The only character that hangs below the baseline in Figure 4.6 is the lowercase "q."

2. Cap height

The **cap height** or **capline** is another imaginary line. This one marks the height of all capital letters in a typeface. Notice that the cap height is below the maximum height of the typeface.

3. Crossbar

A stroke that connects two lines in the capital letterforms of "A" and "H" is called a **crossbar**. A horizontal stroke that does not connect two lines, like the one in the lower case "f" or "t," is known as a **cross stroke**.

---

[11] https://learnable.com/books/jump-start-html5-canvas-and-svg#overview

[12] http://alistapart.com/article/using-svg-for-flexible-scalable-and-fun-backgrounds-part-i

[13] http://css-tricks.com/using-svg/

4. Serif

Serif is the name given to the finishing strokes at the bottoms and tops of certain typefaces. I'll talk more about serifs when we cover typeface distinctions.

5. Mean line

Another imaginary horizontal line that marks the top edge of the lowercase letters is the **mean line** (or **midline**). Contrary to what you might imply from its name, the mean line isn't always exactly centered between the baseline and the cap height.

6. Bowl

The **bowl** of a letter is the rounded curve that encloses negative space in a letterform. Examples of bowls can be seen in the letters "D," "o," and "g."

7. Descender

The lower portion of a lowercase letter (such as "g," "j," "p," "q," and "y") that extends below the baseline of a typeface is known as the **descender**. The only other characters that typically extend below the baseline are the old-style numerals in some typefaces. These types of numerals, examples of which from the Georgia typeface can be seen in Figure 4.7, were thought to blend better with lowercase roman numerals, and they look particularly good when used within a body of text.

1567 1567

Figure 4.7. Old-style numerals in the Georgia font on the left, and standard numerals in Helvetica on the right

8. Counter

The negative space within a letter is called the **counter**. In some letters, like "A," "o," and "P," the counter is fully enclosed. The non-closed negative spaces in letters like "G," "u," and "c" are also known as counters.

9. Stem

A stem is the main vertical or diagonal stroke in a letterform. These include the vertical portions of the letters "I" and "H," as well as all the strokes in the letter "W."

10. Tittle

This is probably my favorite typeface term. **Tittle** is the name given to the dot above the lowercase "j" and "i."

11. Terminal

The end of a stem or stroke that has no serif is known as a **terminal**. Even the ends of some serif typefaces have terminals, as you can see in the letter "c" in Figure 4.6.

12. Ascender

Some lowercase letters have an **ascender**, which is an extension that rises above the mean line. Those letters are "b," "d," "f," "h," "k," "l," and "t."

13. Leg

The lower angled strokes seen in the letters "K," "R," and "Q" are known as legs. These are also sometimes referred to as tails.

14. Ligature

You may have noticed in Figure 4.6 that the "f" and "i" of the word "fix" are combined into one character. This joining of characters is known as a **ligature**. Ligatures are most often seen in serif faces, and exist to give the spacing between certain characters a greater aesthetic balance, as Figure 4.8 illustrates.

Figure 4.8. Example of an "ae" ligature in the font Insignia

15. x-height

Simply put, **x-height** is the vertical space occupied by the lowercase "x" in a given typeface. More accurately, it's the distance between the baseline and mean line that defines the body of lowercase letterforms—excluding ascenders and descenders. X-height is a key factor in typeface identification, and typefaces with larger x-heights are generally regarded as being more readable.

Although it's impractical, you can actually use x-height as a relative unit of measurement in CSS (ex).

Text Spacing

Now that you know how to describe the parts of a letterform, the next step is to be able to define and adjust the space between letters. I mentioned before that many typographic decisions are based on spacing. This is has always been true with printed type, and became applicable to web type with the advent of CSS. Regardless of whether we're talking about using type for print or for the Web, there are two directions in which we can control spacing: horizontally and vertically.

Horizontal Spacing

Kerning and tracking are two terms you'll often hear in conversations about horizontal letter spacing. **Kerning** is the process of adjusting the space between individual letters. Often when you're working with type, you'll notice pairs of letters that appear too close together, or too far apart. Most fonts have a set of rules that determine the spacing between specific characters. The kerning between the letters "Wa," for instance, should be—and is—much tighter than the kerning between "WV." Most of the time, the rules for the font are sufficient to make the text readable. Otherwise, you can adjust the individual letter pairs within your image creation software of choice. Figure 4.9 shows examples of text with no kerning applied, automatic kerning, and manually adjusted kerning.

Figure 4.9. AWE-inspiring kerning examples

For the text in a web page, it's impossible to make letter-by-letter kerning adjustments. What you *can* do is adjust the `letter-spacing` CSS property, which is known in the print world as adjusting the font's **tracking**. Like kerning, tracking adjusts the horizontal spacing between letterforms, but applies to the space between each letter. If you want your text to have a more open, airy feel, try adding a bit of letter spacing as I've done in Figure 4.10.

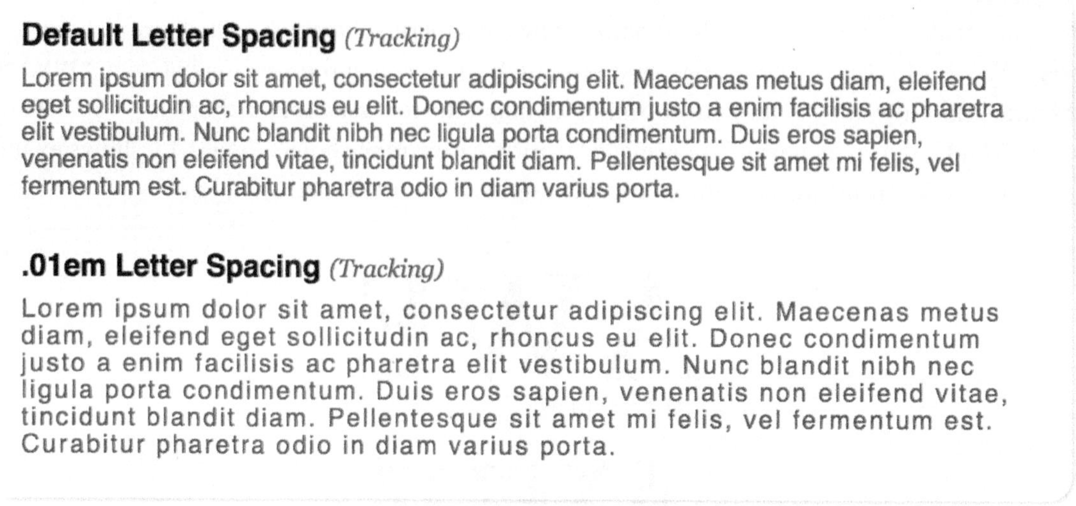

Default Letter Spacing *(Tracking)*

Lorem ipsum dolor sit amet, consectetur adipiscing elit. Maecenas metus diam, eleifend eget sollicitudin ac, rhoncus eu elit. Donec condimentum justo a enim facilisis ac pharetra elit vestibulum. Nunc blandit nibh nec ligula porta condimentum. Duis eros sapien, venenatis non eleifend vitae, tincidunt blandit diam. Pellentesque sit amet mi felis, vel fermentum est. Curabitur pharetra odio in diam varius porta.

.01em Letter Spacing *(Tracking)*

Lorem ipsum dolor sit amet, consectetur adipiscing elit. Maecenas metus diam, eleifend eget sollicitudin ac, rhoncus eu elit. Donec condimentum justo a enim facilisis ac pharetra elit vestibulum. Nunc blandit nibh nec ligula porta condimentum. Duis eros sapien, venenatis non eleifend vitae, tincidunt blandit diam. Pellentesque sit amet mi felis, vel fermentum est. Curabitur pharetra odio in diam varius porta.

Figure 4.10. Letter spacing example

Another horizontal spacing option in CSS is provided by the word-spacing property. This property can take a positive or negative length, or the keyword normal. As you might expect, it affects the amount of whitespace between words.

Vertical Spacing

In print design language, the vertical space between lines of text is known as **leading**. This term comes from the early days of letterpress when blank strips of lead were used to separate lines of metal type. When there were no added spacers, the lines were said to be set "solid." Text with added vertical space is much easier to read. As you can see in the first paragraph in Figure 4.11, the default spacing between lines of text is too small. Ideally, you want the line height on your body copy to be about one-and-a-half times the size of your text; so if you have 12px text, 18px is a good readable line height. In the second paragraph we've adjusted the CSS line-height property to 1.5em. An em is a CSS unit that measures the size of a font, from the top of a font's cap height to the bottom of its lowest descender. Originally, the em was equal to the width of the capital letter M, which is where its name came from.

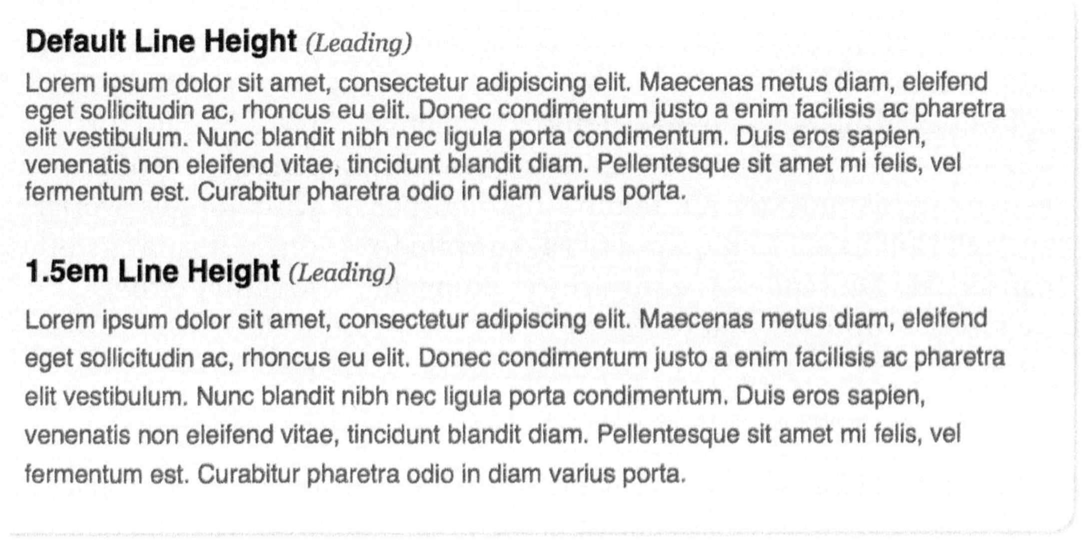

Default Line Height *(Leading)*

Lorem ipsum dolor sit amet, consectetur adipiscing elit. Maecenas metus diam, eleifend eget sollicitudin ac, rhoncus eu elit. Donec condimentum justo a enim facilisis ac pharetra elit vestibulum. Nunc blandit nibh nec ligula porta condimentum. Duis eros sapien, venenatis non eleifend vitae, tincidunt blandit diam. Pellentesque sit amet mi felis, vel fermentum est. Curabitur pharetra odio in diam varius porta.

1.5em Line Height *(Leading)*

Lorem ipsum dolor sit amet, consectetur adipiscing elit. Maecenas metus diam, eleifend eget sollicitudin ac, rhoncus eu elit. Donec condimentum justo a enim facilisis ac pharetra elit vestibulum. Nunc blandit nibh nec ligula porta condimentum. Duis eros sapien, venenatis non eleifend vitae, tincidunt blandit diam. Pellentesque sit amet mi felis, vel fermentum est. Curabitur pharetra odio in diam varius porta.

Figure 4.11. Leading example

Text Alignment

Have you ever noticed that the text you see in books and magazines is often aligned along both the left- and right-hand sides of the page or column? This type of text alignment is known is **justification**. When text is justified, the letter and word spacing is automatically adjusted so that each full line of text has a word or letter that lines up against the left and right edges of the text area. Many print designers will use justified text for any text block that's over two lines long and is wide enough. You can take this same text treatment to the Web with CSS by setting the `text-alignment` property to `justify`. Before you go and justify the whole Internet, though, let me give you two warnings about justified text:

A river runs through it

Occasionally, a gap created by wider spacing in one justified row will line up with a gap in the next row, and the next, and the next… and you end up with a canyon or **river** in your type, as shown in Figure 4.12. This can be distracting for the reader. Print designers can makes adjustments to fix this sort of problem, but on the Web, it's difficult to predict and impossible to fix.

What? Are? You? Saying?

The river problem is even more pronounced with narrow columns. Words will often be isolated against the left and right margin, or stretched over the entire width of the column. Most word processing programs fix this problem by hyphenating words where necessary. Browsers are unable to do this kind of auto-hyphenation, so web designers should avoid using justified text in narrow spaces.

Lorem ipsum dolor sit amet, consectetuer adipiscing elit, sed diam nonummy nibh euimoda tindant laoreet dolore magana alieuam volutpat. Ut wisi enim ad minim veniam, quis nos exerci tation ullamcorper suscipit lobortista aliquip ex ea commodo consequat. Duisaut vel eum iriure dolor in hendrerit vulputate velit esse.

Justified text and narrow columns, particularly narrow columns with longer words do not play well together either.

Figure 4.12. Justification problems: can you spot the three other rivers present in this lorem ipsum text?

If you don't want to change the `text-alignment` of your text to `justify`, your other options are `left`, `right`, or `center`. When text is centered or aligned along the left or right edge of the page or column, the spacing between the characters and words remains constant. The river problem can occur with any text block, but it's much less likely to cause legibility issues in text that's centered or justified on one side only.

If you want to see how some HTML text will look in the browser with different leading, tracking, and alignment settings applied, two great tools to check out are Marko Dugonjic's Typetester[14] and Panduka Senaka's Typechart.[15] Both of these web applications enable you to try out a variety of typographic configurations for HTML text, and then grab the CSS needed to create the effect.

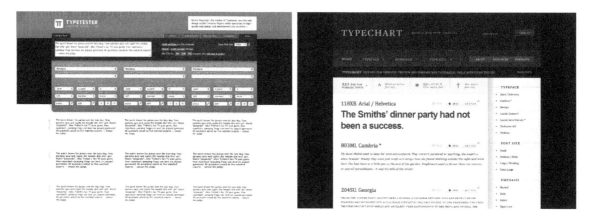

Figure 4.13. Typetester (left) and Typechart (right) allow you to quickly test-drive HTML type configurations

Typeface Distinctions

Everybody knows what a font is. It's a set of letters that appear in a certain style; they come pre-installed on your computer. And you change the font when you want your text to look different.

---

[14] http://www.typetester.org/
[15] http://www.typechart.com/

The average Windows PC has just over 40 fonts installed by default, while the average Mac user has access to around 100 fonts. Many of these fonts are grouped together into font families, with each font within the family representing a different variation of the core font. Most font families include the regular font face, along with italic, bold, and bold italic variants. Some fonts have no variations at all; some may only have bold or italic, and some commercially available font families have hundreds of variants.

Just as all the members of some families have big ears or abnormally long pinkie toes, every font family has its own unique, identifiable characteristics. Take a look at the variation that exists between fonts for the letter "g" in Figure 4.14.

These characteristics are what help us to categorize fonts and font families. The majority of font families can be classified as either serif or sans-serif. Of the 14 different fonts represented in Figure 4.14, seven could be classified as serif and seven as sans-serif. Can you distinguish between them? Beyond this distinction, there are many other ways in which we can classify and group fonts. I prefer to group fonts into six simple categories: serif, sans-serif, handwritten, monospace, novelty, and dingbats. Let's look at each of them now.

Figure 4.14. Fourteen Gs

Serif Fonts

Historians believe that the serif has its origin in Roman stone carving. There is much debate over the original purpose of these ornamental strokes, but in more recent history, they've been proven to increase legibility in large blocks of text by providing a horizontal line of reference. When designers choose a serif font, Times New Roman is often the first one that comes to mind. However, there's a great variety of serif fonts on offer. To help us with that decision, it's a good idea to first decide what type of *voice* we want our text to have.

Take a look at the Garamond text in Figure 4.15. Garamond is an **old-style serif** font. Old-style serif fonts are adapted from the brushstrokes of Italian scribes and can be recognized both by the smooth transitions between thick and thin strokes, and by their rounded serif edges. When I see an old-style serif font, it exudes historic, handcrafted charm. At the same time, fonts like Garamond are extremely versatile: they're not so old-fashioned that they're unusable in modern applications.

Figure 4.15. Serif categories

The second font in Figure 4.15 is Baskerville, a **transitional serif** font. The curved angle that connects the terminal of the stroke to the serif is known as a **bracket**. The brackets of transitional serif fonts are rounded, but the edges of the serifs are squared off. The simple addition of 90-degree angles and perfectly straight lines gives this category of font a more modern and mechanical voice. This category of serif fonts is known as transitional because it provides a transition between old-style and modern serif fonts.

The third font, Didot, is a **modern serif** font. Modern serif fonts provide a large amount of contrast between the thick and thin strokes, and their serifs are often completely unbracketed. Modern serif fonts were introduced during the Industrial Revolution as a radical alternative to the transitional serif style. Today, these fonts have an association with elegance, sophistication, and fashion. They represent timelessness more than cutting-edge modernity. Because of their fine line details, modern serif fonts are really only suitable for use in headlines. The consistent use of Italian Didot in *Vogue* magazine,[16] as seen in Figure 4.16, helped to establish both the font and the magazine as icons of style. Other famous magazines that use modern serif font faces for their mastheads include *Brides*, *W*, *Elle*, *Parents*, *Seventeen*, and *Harper's Bazaar*. They're fairly uncommon in web design, but are certainly a classy choice if high style is what you're aiming for.

[16] http://www.vogue.com/

Figure 4.16. Modern serifs lending a classy feel to Vogue

In the later part of the 1800s, as advertising, posters, and flyers became more common, a bolder variation of modern serif fonts was needed to catch people's attention. It was at this time that **slab serif** fonts were first introduced. Slab serif faces like Rockwell have an industrial but friendly voice that's far less snooty than modern serifs, and even more contemporary. Because most slab serifs were designed to be readable from a distance, they make for excellent headlines and have been very popular on the Web lately. Figure 4.17 shows a couple of beautiful examples of slab serifs in action. On the left *The Sew Weekly*'s[17] logo features a typeface called Brosse. On the right we have *The Mid-century Modernist*,[18] which uses Rockwell Light for its logo. I personally think that slab serifs tend to feel masculine. The Sew Weekly is a beautiful contradiction to that notion, and evidence that you can go against convention when choosing fonts.

---

[17] http://www.sewweekly.com/
[18] http://midcenturymodernist.com/

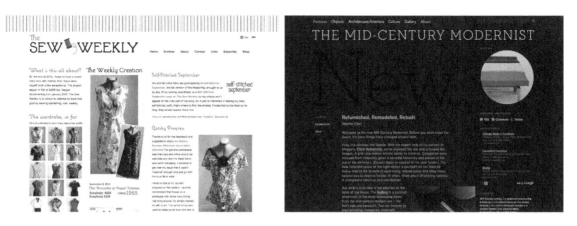

Figure 4.17. Slab serifs at the Mid-century Modernist and Sew Weekly

Sans–serif Fonts

At the time when typographers began experimenting with slab serifs, the idea of eliminating the serif altogether seemed like a huge mistake. Serifs were a tradition, so removing them was typographic castration. The initial sans-serif fonts were so loathed in the 1800s that they were referred to as grotesque. Eventually, though, people began to warm to the idea of serif-less typefaces, and by the 1920s some speculated that the serif would soon be eliminated.

Although serif fonts are still used extensively, the popularity and versatility of the sans-serif font category continues to grow. These types of fonts have a cleaner and more contemporary feel. They stand out as headlines, especially when paired with body text that's set in a serif face. This has long been a standard practice in print design, and is a tip that I was taught in college for creating contrast between headlines and body copy. On the Web, though, the roles have been reversed for a very long time. This is mainly due to the one-two punch of low-resolution display hardware, combined with poor text hinting and rendering in older operating systems. Because of the stroke variation and minute detail of serif fonts, they can become almost unreadable at small sizes on lower-resolution displays. As the pixel density of displays increase and older computers die off, we're free to serif, or not to serif. Figure 4.18 shows Spoongraphics,[19] a design blog I enjoy following, which uses the time-honored tradition of sans-serif headings and serif body copy.

---

[19] http://blog.spoongraphics.co.uk/

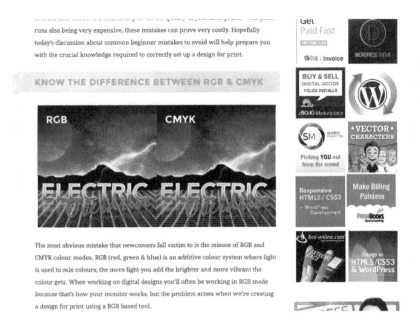

Figure 4.18. An Example From Spoongraphics

Regardless of how they're used, sans-serif fonts are extremely legible and practical for almost any purpose. The most ubiquitous sans-serif fonts on the Web are Arial and Verdana. Each of these font families exists in the default font sets of both major operating systems, and, as a result, they're predictably the workhorses of web body copy. In the design world, these families have a reputation for being overused and generic (and in the design community, Arial has the added stigma of being widely considered the poor cousin of Helvetica). This makes Arial and Verdana great for body text, where voiceless legibility is the goal, but for headlines and artistic applications, a more characterful feel is often required. Sometimes a stronger serif font, or a more distinguished sans-serif, will do the trick, but there are certainly many more options available outside these two categories.

Handwritten Fonts

Before the invention of movable type systems, all text had to be carved, brushed, or written by hand. The downside to handwritten text—especially my own—is that achieving a uniformity of letterforms, alignment, and spacing can be frustrating. And, as a result of these challenges, handwritten text can be very difficult to read. Yet the wonderful aspect about handwriting is that it acts as a symbol of humanity, giving a tangible personality to the text it represents. Just look at the text in Figure 4.19. Each line was written to represent the personality of the font in which it's written.

Handwritten fonts provide a personal touch without the human error factor. The lettering and alignment in a handwritten font will be consistent, and if the font is well-designed, the spacing should be good, too. As you look around at handwritten fonts on the Web, you'll probably start to think that anyone and their cousin's dog could create one, and it's true. Unlike serif and sans-serif faces that require practice and precision, handwritten fonts are all about personality. If you want to create a font from your own handwriting, there are dozens of tools and services out there. One of the simplest sites for this is YourFonts.com.[20] You simply print out a PDF template, scribble your glyphs into the little boxes, scan it, upload it, and for a small fee, you can download an OpenType format font file.

If you're trying to make a website feel very friendly and human, sometimes a font, even a handwritten one, is a little too perfect. Take the Packdog Website[21] in Figure 4.20, for example. If you look closely at the lettering, you'll notice that no two letters are exactly the same. That's because rather than being a font, it's a beautiful example of hand lettering. Most people probably would fail to notice the subtle variation between the same letters here, but that tiny detail helps this conference website feel a lot more fun and friendly.

Shall we visit the Winery?
Bickham Script Pro

Cake Baker
LHF Cosmic Cursive

Fresh Artichokes
ArtBrush

STRAIGHT UP GANGSTA
Bring tha noize

Figure 4.19. Handwritten fonts: for a human touch

---

[20] http://yourfonts.com
[21] http://chirp.twitter.com/

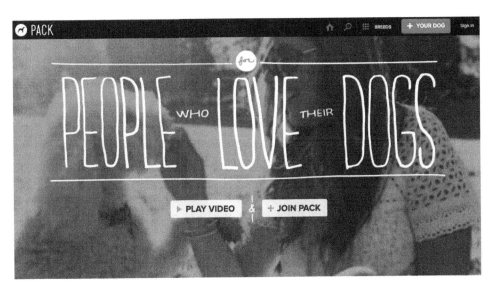

Figure 4.20. Hand lettering on the Packdog.com site

Fixed-width Fonts

You may have noticed by now that in most fonts, each letter takes up a different amount of space. For instance, the capital "W" takes up a large area, while the letter "l" has a very narrow footprint. To illustrate this point in plain text, take a guess which of the sentences in Figure 4.21 has more characters.

Women of the world wear makeup.
The lily in the valley is tiny.

Figure 4.21. A proportionately spaced font

That was a trick question; they actually have the same number of characters! So why does the first sentence appear so much longer than the second? The explanation for this phenomenon is that the majority of fonts are proportionately spaced. Associated with each character of each font are rules that determine not only the width of the character, but also the amount of space that will appear around each character. Take a look at those two sentences again, this time displayed in the Courier font, in Figure 4.22.

```
Women of the world wear makeup.
The lily in the valley is tiny.
```

Figure 4.22. A fixed-width or monospaced font

The reason the two sentences appear to be the same width now is that Courier is a fixed-width or monospaced font. This category of fonts has uniform spacing, and the letterforms are designed so that they're similar in width. Fixed-width fonts were initially designed around the technical limitations of typewriters. Since early typewriters were incapable of moving the typed page a different distance when a "w" was typed, rather than an "i," specialized fonts were developed for these devices. These fonts had to remain readable, despite the spacing being the same for every letter. Early computer displays employed fixed-width fonts as well, but it was only a short time before computers were able to display much more legible variable-width (or proportional) fonts.

So why are fixed-width fonts still around today? Mainly for the sanity of coders and accountants. When you have to write code or display data as text, it's important that characters line up from row to row and column to column. If you're reading this book, you're probably already familiar with fixed-width fonts from writing HTML and CSS. The benefits of these monspaced faces can be seen clearly in Figure 4.23. CSS3, please![22] is a cross-browser CSS3 rule generator that allows you to experiment with CSS3 properties.

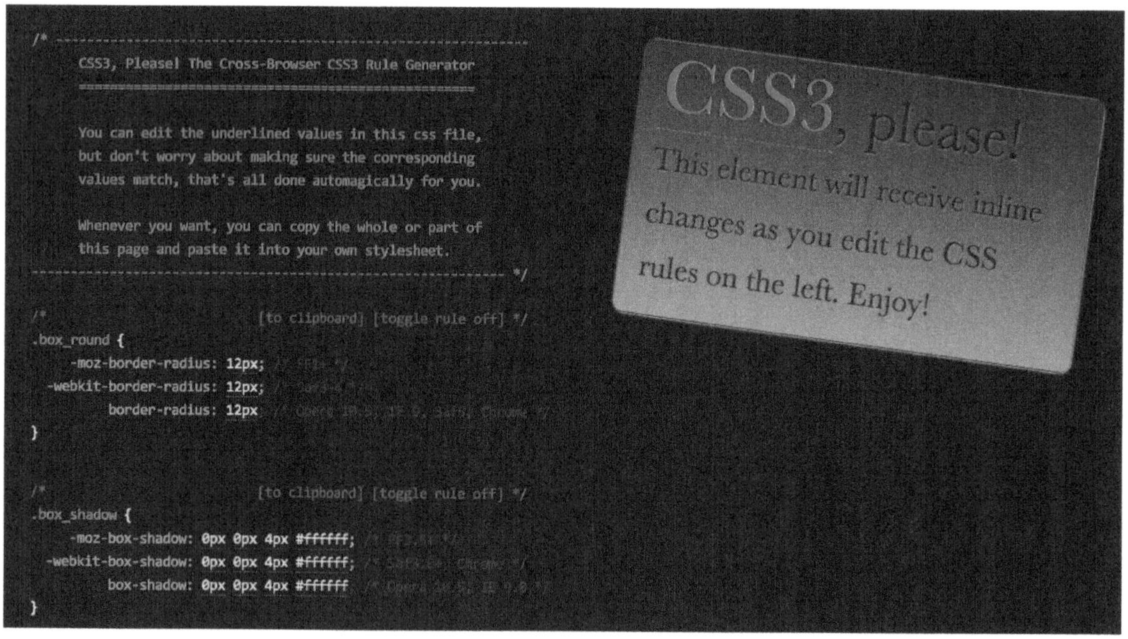

Figure 4.23. Fixed-width fonts in action at CSS3, please!

On the Web, the standard way to display text in a fixed-width font is to wrap it with `<pre>` and `</pre>` tags. `pre` is short for preformatted text, and aside from displaying fixed-width characters, the `pre` element also preserves tabs, spaces, and line breaks. This usually makes displaying code or tabular data on a website as simple as cutting and pasting from the source. I say *usually* because HTML tags that exist within preformatted text will be rendered normally, so if you're trying to include any tags in your code, you'll need to replace any <s with the HTML character code equivalent of

---

[22] http://css3please.com/

`<`, and any >s with `>`. As with every other HTML element, `pre` can be styled with CSS. Often, web developers who plan to show code on a page want the code to stand out from the regular text. Using CSS, the `pre` tag can be given a border, a background treatment, additional margins, or a different text treatment to help it to stand out.

Another interesting, albeit obsolete, use of fixed-width fonts is in the creation of ASCII art. ASCII (American Standard Code for Information Interchange) was one of the original English character encodings for communications equipment, and for several years the 95 printable characters in this seven-bit system were the only graphics that ever showed up on a display. Before the Internet existed outside of the military and academia, there were networks of dial-up bulletin board systems (BBSs), many of which displayed menus and game graphics in ASCII characters. Having grown up during the peak of the BBS era, I loved to see the "underground" graphics people could create using only fixed-width type.

Although you can now create more intricate ASCII art with web apps like ASCII-O-Matic[23] or Patrick Gillespie's Text Ascii Art Generator,[24] the ASCII art created during the late 1980s and early 1990s was composed character by character, and really pushed the limits of the medium. This type of artwork, like the Energy BBS title in Figure 4.24, is an often-overlooked link in the history of computer graphics.

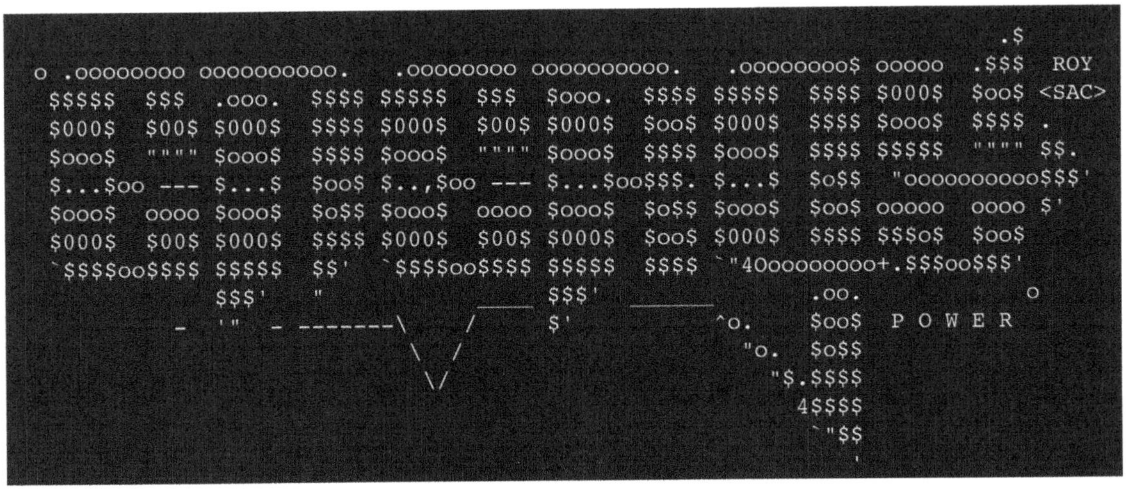

Figure 4.24. Energy BBS ASCII art by Carsten Cumbrowski

[23] http://www.typorganism.com/asciiomatic/

[24] http://patorjk.com/software/taag/

Novelty Fonts

Novelty fonts, which are also known as **display**, **decorative**, or **fantasy** fonts, represent the vast majority of free fonts that are available online. Some of the fonts in this category are modified versions of popular serif or sans-serif fonts, and some are completely off-the-wall ideas that would be better described as conceptual art than a font face. By their very nature, these fonts are less legible than their traditional counterparts, but when used sparingly, they can add a wealth of personality and flair to a design. A few examples of novelty fonts are shown in Figure 4.25.

Sometimes, a good place to use a novelty font is as a starting block for a logo design. Take a look at Tony Yoo's personal portfolio site Hype-nation[25] in Figure 4.26. It's a bold, retro, geometric design that works well with the blocky typeface that he's used for the logo. It looks a lot like the capital letters from a font called La Moda, but most likely it was customized to give it a personal touch.

KUNG PAO CHICKEN?
Chinese Takeaway

give me the monkey
BlackCasper

Vowel Movement
Squealer Embossed

BUT IT'S STILL JULY
Almonte Snow

GRITS & GRAVY
Burnstown Dam

Figure 4.25. Examples of novelty fonts

Figure 4.26. Hype-nation's bold retro design

While I do know a thing or two about typefaces, I'm hardly a font-recognizing machine. Usually, if I come across an interesting string of text in a font I fail to recognize, the first thing I think is WTF! I am, of course, referring to MyFont's excellent WhatTheFont[26] automatic font identification system. All you have to do is crop and clean up a block of type, upload it to WTF, and it will search for character matches in its database. Figure 4.27 shows some of the matches for the Hype-nation text above. WTF really is an invaluable tool, and if it fails to recognize your text, the site has a forum of "cloak-draped font enthusiasts" who love to solve typographic puzzles.

Figure 4.27. MyFonts' WhatTheFont service

As with all design choices, before you use a novelty font, you should think about your client's requirements and target audience. Most clients will already have some form of branding in place, and choosing a bizarre or offbeat novelty font may tarnish the company's image. Even so, it's best to keep an open mind when you're coming up with themes for a website design. It may be that the company you're working with wants to stray from its corporate image.

Dingbat Fonts

When you're looking for illustrations and artwork to incorporate into the design of a website, you should consider **dingbat** or **symbol** fonts. In the early days of print, dingbats were ornamental characters used to separate printed text and fill whitespace. Original dingbat fonts consisted mainly

---

[26] http://new.myfonts.com/WhatTheFont/

of flourishes and commonly used symbols; however, the concept of dingbat fonts changed radically with the digital font revolution. Now, any series of graphics can be assigned as characters in a dingbat font.

While these fonts may not be of much use from a typesetting perspective, they can be useful as supportive vector graphics and icons. Since fonts consist of scalable vector shapes, dingbat glyphs can be converted to outlines in Photoshop or Illustrator, and then resized, dismantled, and manipulated without any loss of quality. The only issue when using these fonts is that you have to know where to find the glyph you're after. Occasionally, I'll remember an arrow or symbol from a dingbat font, and type out half the alphabet before I find the one I want. Fortunately, though, most dingbat fonts have a theme, so it's easy to remember which font the glyph is in, even if the specific character is hard to find.

When people think about dingbats, the first sets that come to mind are Wingdings and Webdings, the dingbat fonts that come pre-installed in Windows. There are actually hundreds of other dingbat fonts available on the Web. A few examples are given in Figure 4.28.

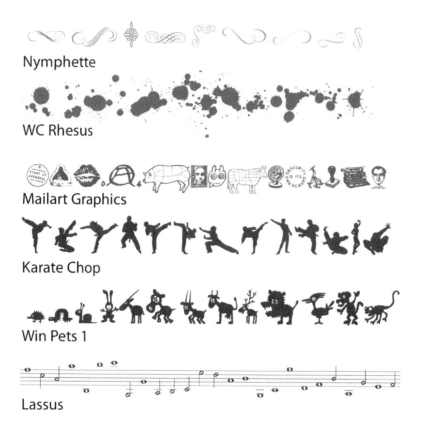

Figure 4.28. A few examples of free dingbat fonts

Finding Fonts

Although I've mentioned that you can find fonts on the Web a few times now, I've yet to really give you any places to look for them. If you start googling for fonts, you'll probably discover that there are three main categories of font sites out there: free font galleries, commercial font galleries, and sites for individual artists and foundries. All are great sources of fonts to add to your typographic tool belt.

Free Font Galleries

These websites list and categorize free fonts from many designers. Some of the designers listed on these galleries have their own websites, through which they sell other fonts that they've designed. If you enjoy the fonts created by particular designers, be sure to track down the rest of their work. Remember that there are a lot of really ugly free fonts out there, and while many websites claim to offer free fonts, you often have to wade through loads of annoying ads to download them. Also, if you plan to embed a font (even a free one) into your site using `@font-face`, be sure that the font's license allows it. With that said, here are a few great resources for free fonts:

- Font Squirrel, at http://fontsquirrel.com/
- The League of Movable Type, at https://www.theleagueofmoveabletype.com/
- DaFont, at http://dafont.com/

Commercial Font Galleries

Like the free and shareware galleries mentioned above, these websites promote fonts from many different designers and foundries. But unlike those galleries, most of the fonts here cost money. In most cases, though, you really get what you pay for with typography. If you license a font from one of these sites, as well as gaining a complete set of characters, the purchased fonts often include bold, italic, oblique, and other variants.

- FontShop, at http://fontshop.com/
- Monotype, at http://fonts.com/
- Veer, at http://veer.com/products/fonts/
- MyFonts, at http://myfonts.com/
- Adobe Fonts, at http://adobe.com/type/

Individual Artists and Foundries

Many of my favorite contemporary fonts come from a handful of individual artists and companies. Most of these websites have a few free fonts, as well as offering fonts for sale:

- Jos Buivenga's exljbris Font Foundry, at http://www.exljbris.com/. Creator of such popular typefaces as Museo, Anivers, and Diavlo.

- Letterhead Fonts, at http://letterheadfonts.com. This little foundry has over 200 high-quality unique fonts from which to choose.

- Blue Vinyl Fonts by Jess Latham, at http://bvfonts.com/. Like many font designers, Jess started designing fonts as a hobby. His freeware and paid fonts have a unique style and are very well done.

- Fountain Type by Peter Bruhn, at http://fountaintype.com/. Fountain features some of the best fonts from about 20-odd designers around the world. The site also provides attractive freeware fonts.

- Typodermic Fonts by Ray Larabie, at http://typodermicfonts.com/. Ray is a rock star in the realm of free fonts. His work is known for having large character sets that are top quality.

- Misprinted Type by Eduardo Recife, at http://misprintedtype.com/. Eduardo is the man when it comes to weathered, worn, and eclectic font faces. His work is unmistakably unique, if a little twisted.

- Pizzadude by Jakob Fischer, at http://pizzadude.dk/. Jakob has an admittedly goofy and laid-back style, but has cranked out over 500 handmade fonts since 1998.

Choosing the Right Fonts

Even if you understand all the technical aspects of letterforms and typeface categories, and have access to all the fonts in the world, you can still have difficulty choosing the right ones. That's because font selection is based just as heavily on artistic license and emotional association as it is on technical issues. So, where do we begin?

In order to start your quest for the perfect font, you should first define the feelings you're trying to evoke in your target audience. Are you trying to show that the company the website represents is hip and young, or would you rather portray an aura of steadfast wisdom? Do you want to create a site based on a certain theme, like a Hawaiian luau or a Mexican fiesta, or are you trying to convey a more formal identity? By asking yourself these kinds of questions, and thinking about fonts on an emotional level, you should be able to decide reasonably easily whether a given font is appropriate for your application.

If you're unable to answer those questions about a particular font, make up your own questions. Take a look at the screenshot from G'nosh[27] in Figure 4.29. What questions do you think the designers of that site asked themselves as they were choosing the fonts for it? Obviously they were going for a handwritten feel, but why? I'm guessing they wanted to establish a brand that was as casual and approachable as possible.

---

[27] http://www.gnosh.co.uk/

Figure 4.29. The casual and approachable G'nosh's website

Think about it, you've seen billions of letters and millions of words in your lifetime; so, whether you know it or not, you already have some emotional connections on which you can base your font choices. Think back to the logos, the album covers, the textbooks, and the signage you've seen. How have those typographic elements affected your perception of the entities they represent?

Now, let's take that idea and work backwards, using a generic entity like Joe's Restaurant. The font that you choose for this design will play a crucial role in the way potential diners perceive the attitude and identity of the restaurant. Take a look at Figure 4.30, and try to choose some fonts that make you think of a casual Italian bistro. Okay, now pick fonts that suggest a metropolitan restaurant serving five-star cuisine. How about a tacky dockside bar? There's no right answer for any of these scenarios, but there are definitely some fonts that will outright fail to work in each case. First, try to narrow the field down to a few good candidates, and then try to refine your choices again, until you find one that works well.

Joe's Restaurant Skia	Joe's Restaurant Versailles	*Joe's Restaurant* Legault	Joe's Restaurant Colona MT
JOE'S RESTAURANT Lithos Pro	JOE'S RESTAURANT Charlemagne	*Joe's Restaurant* Park Avenue	Joe's Restaurant Disgusting Behavior
JOE'S RESTAURANT Umbra	Joe's Restaurant Amigo	*Joe's Restaurant* Sloop	Joe's Restaurant Bubbledot ICG
Joe's Restaurant Insignia	Joe's Restaurant Adobe Jenson Pro	*Joe's Restaurant* Pelican	JOE'S RESTAURANT Cottonwood
Joe's Restaurant Bauhaus 93	Joe's Restaurant Modern No. 20	Joe's Restaurant Harrington	joe's restaurant Slugfest

Figure 4.30. 20 different fonts to make you want to eat at Joe's

Remember that there are no bad fonts, just inappropriate ones. While a particular font might fail to work for one purpose, it may strike just the right chord in another situation. The trick is to try to keep an open mind. If you can narrow the field to a few possibilities, try asking a friend or co-worker the question, "Which one makes you feel more [adjective]?", inserting the feeling you're aiming to elicit.

Finally, when you're choosing fonts, it's important to limit your selection. As a rule of thumb, try to use at least two, but no more than four different fonts in a website design. Before incorporating a new font, remember that you probably have some variants (bold, italic, condensed, black, regular, and so on) at your disposal to vary your type while maintaining consistency. Try to also avoid combining two different serif fonts or two different sans-serif fonts in the same project. Like the discordant colors phenomenon I talked about in Chapter 2, placing different fonts from the same family next to each other in a design can feel eerily uncomfortable.

Setting Font Size and Line Height

The size of text is—and always has been—a confusing topic. Over 300 years had elapsed in the history of printed type before the French typefounder Père Sébastien Truchet introduced the typographic point. Although points have been the standard units of measurement for typography ever since, the exact size of this *standard* unit has changed several times throughout history, due to differences between the English and French units of measurement. It was only with the onset of digital typography that the official size of the point was set to 1/72 of an inch.

Setting the size of text on the Web has had an equally shaky past. While the size of type in the print world is measured by points, the size of type on the Web is relative to the resolution of the viewer's monitor and can be set in various types of units. The most popular units for setting text on the web are pixels, points, %, and ems. Without going too deeply into it, it's easiest to say that 16px = 12pt = 100% = 1em. In CSS, the pixel (px) is the smallest—and best—relative unit for setting the size of text. Monitor resolution is set in pixels, as are the dimensions of all display graphics, so it makes sense to control text size with pixels, as well. So, why doesn't everyone set web text sizes in pixels?

Well, mainly because some browsers don't allow text that's set in pixels to be scaled. This is potentially an accessibility problem for users unable to read small text. I say it's *potentially* a problem, because most browsers now give users the option to zoom the page rather than having to try to increase the font size. If you want to ensure that the text in your site is scalable as well as zoomable, you can set your text in ems.

Because I think in pixels, my current approach to setting font size and line height on the Web follows the logic of Wilson Miner's 2007 *A List Apart* article, "Setting Type on the Web to a Baseline Grid."[28] Like our vertical, column-based grids, a baseline grid is a set of equally spaced horizontal lines which your text should line up with. Following a baseline grid helps give your content a sense of rhythm instead of feeling arbitrarily placed. The main concept in Wilson's article is that you remove the default margin and padding from all elements, set your `font-size` and `line-height` in the `body` element, then give all elements a `line-height` and a bottom margin that either matches or is a multiple of your `body` `line-height`. It sounds complicated, but it's really quite easy.

Using Punctuation and Special Characters

When you type text into any relatively modern word-processing program, you see nice "curly" opening and closing punctuation marks when you hit the double quotation marks key. Curly quotation marks can't be found on your keyboard, as Figure 4.31 shows; however, word-processing programs understand that when you put words in quotes, you want nice left and right quotes, and it replaces the characters you typed in with the correct ones. The same goes with apostrophes. Have you ever seen an ASCII apostrophe like the one on your keyboard in a book or brochure? Of course not. What we usually see in printed material is a closing single quotation mark. In fact, a vast array of characters are unrepresented on a standard keyboard, even though these characters show up on web pages and in printed material.

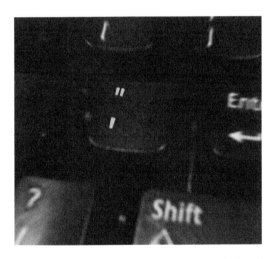

Figure 4.31. The quotation mark key on a standard keyboard

Now, that's all well and good for people using word processors. For those of us typing text into an HTML document, though, there's no system to automatically replace the characters from our keyboards with the grammatically correct equivalents. Depending on which type of character encoding your website uses, when you paste these characters directly into an HTML document, you may see a bunch of gibberish on the rendered page. Additionally, the inclusion in text of characters that are used by HTML, like < and >, will wreak havoc in your page, as they'll be interpreted as the beginning or ending of an HTML tag.

---

[28] http://www.alistapart.com/articles/settingtypeontheweb

For these reasons, a series of special codes or **entities** has been created; we type these into our HTML documents to produce correct punctuation marks and just about any special character that we could need. The examples in Table 4.1 are just a sample of the many HTML character codes that exist. The code on the far left is known as an entity name or keyword. For instance, to produce a copyright symbol in your document, enter © directly into your HTML, and you'll see a © in the rendered page. Each of these entities also has a numerical equivalent; for © it's #169, so © will produce the same symbol. For a more complete list of codes and their alternative entity numbers, check out W3Schools HTML entities page.[29]

Table 4.1. Sample list of HTML character entity references

Entity	Character	Description
&lt;	<	Less than
&gt;	>	Greater than
&amp;	&	Ampersand
&lsquo;	'	Left single quote
&rsquo;	'	Right single quote
&ldquo;	"	Left double quote
&rdquo;	"	Right double quote
&laquo;	«	Left angle quote
&raquo;	»	Right angle quote
&reg;	®	Registered trademark
&trade;	™	Trademark
&copy;	©	Copyright
&cent;	¢	Cent
&pound;	£	Pound
&yen;	¥	Yen
&frac14;	¼	One-quarter
&frac12;	½	One-half
&frac34;	¾	Three-quarters

Application: The Fine Print

Type is an important part of the Knoxville Reflexology Group logo. The typeface needed to be strong and have a bold presence, while being clean and friendly. The type uses a combination of Frutiger LT 45 Light and Frutiger LT 65 Bold. This combination of thick and thin typefaces gives a strong sense of contrast, but as both typefaces are from the same family, it helps to unify the logo.

---

[29] http://www.w3schools.com/tags/ref_entities.asp

Figure 4.32. KRG typography in the logo

For the headlines and body copy throughout the KRG site, is was important to chose a quality web font that was sans serif to maximize legibility, and to have a few different weights. Source Sans Pro Bold was used for the headlines and Source Sans Pro Light was selected for the body text. This is mainly because KRG wanted to maintain a modern, sleek look. The body text needed to have an open, inviting feel, so the line height was increased for legibility and to lighten the mood of the site.

The home page needed to draw the visitor in with the latest news, while offering other content to explore. It also needed to be informative, covering different procedures and providing price information. Certain elements, such as prices, could be made to stand out using special CSS classes dedicated just for those purposes. Headlines needed to be clean and bold, with contrasting supportive text.

Therapeutic Reflexology

Reflexology is a science that deals with certain reflex points that correspond to organs, glands, muscles and parts of the body. Reflexology also improves circulation and nerve function while bringing equilibrium and relaxation to the body. Reflexology can be performed on the feet, hands, face and ears.

Learn More

PEMF

Pulsed electro-magnetic field (PEMF) therapy is FDA approved and has been proven to have neurological, physiological and psychological benefits. The PEMF Therapy improves circulation, increases oxygen, reduces swelling, helps the body activate stem cells and increases the body's natural healing and regeneration dramatically.

Learn More

Thermography

A non-invasive way to gain insight to your patient's body and see problem areas. Medical DITI's major clinical value is in its high sensitivity to pathology in the vascular, muscular, neural and skeletal systems and as such can contribute to the pathogenesis and diagnosis made by the clinician.

Learn More

Figure 4.33. Source Sans Pro font used on body copy

The fonts themselves were implemented using `@font-face`, and the fonts are hosted at the site to provide maximum consistency. As you can see in Figure 4.34 below, the text has plenty of room to breathe. The menu has plenty of contrast, the news slider has a bold headline that gets your attention while making it easy to read. The text shadow in the callout box below the slider has a text shadow applied to it with CSS, which adds a slight variation to the rest of the layout.

Figure 4.34. KRG home page design

We will take a look at the final details of the KRG site later. First, we need to learn about imagery: where to find it, what to look for, and how to make it rock your client's socks off.

Chapter

5

Imagery

From layout, to color, to texture, to type, I've been talking about imagery since the beginning of this book. So why should there be a chapter dedicated to imagery alone, right at the end? As with typography, there are many practical concerns related to imagery—including file-type choices, image resolution, and photography sources—that we need to cover. But, naturally, there are also artistic aspects to this topic, and these deserve some detailed discussion.

Figure 5.1. The Camera Eye

The process of choosing photographic, iconic, and illustrative elements for a website design requires a basic understanding of the design principles I covered in the first few chapters. Take Figure 5.1, for instance. I wanted to use an image of a camera at the top of this page as an iconic representation of the subject. However, when I was looking for a suitable picture, my decision was based more on the angle of the image than the type of camera pictured. The direction that the camera faces in this picture greatly affects the sense of movement in this page. If the camera were facing straight ahead, the page would look just fine, but it would *feel* static. If it were facing off to the right, your eye would gravitate off the page rather than into the content. This phenomenon is due to the rules of emphasis that I talked about in Chapter 1. The placement of the camera at the top of this page helps to ensure it will be noticed. Isolating the image makes it stand out even more as a focal point. Finally, the direction of the lens creates a line of continuance that determines the next focal point of the page.

By the end of this chapter, you'll understand these concepts, and know how to apply them to your own designs.

What to Look For

The old adage that a picture is worth a thousand words certainly holds true on the Web. Photographs and illustrations often serve as visual lures that catch passing visitors and reel them into your content. On the other hand, the wrong images, or even a poor presentation of the right ones, can be detrimental to a website's appeal. Every viewer of a photograph or illustration sees that image differently, depending on the person's own background and individual experience. So the thousand words that one person draws from an image may be different from the thousand words another person takes from it.

Before you choose an image or illustration to include in the layout or content of a website, ask yourself the following three questions:

Is it relevant?

Relevant images can add interest to your design and enhance the content of a web page. They provide visual bookmarks that help visitors remember what was covered on the page, and where to look when they return. Take a look at the promo page for Grovemade[1]'s hand-made products in Figure 5.2. The background photograph is visually compelling and relevant, giving the page a workshop vibe and personality that another image may be unable to replicate. This is a logical rule that most people get right when they choose images for content; however, relevance is only one factor to consider when choosing an image.

Figure 5.2. Grovemade's hand-made products

---

[1] http://grovemade.com/

Is it interesting?

Although it's important to maintain a connection between the visual elements of a design and its content, you should avoid always making it priority number one. The problem with looking for relevant imagery is that we often become caught in the trap of being too literal. And when it comes to choosing images, the land of literal is where all clichés are born.

If you were designing a website for a Tex-Mex restaurant, what type of image would you immediately choose? I think my gut instinct would be "happy people eating nachos." This is definitely not an image you'll find on the Tijuana Flats[2] website in Figure 5.3. Instead, you're treated to an atmosphere that's completely unexpected—an old fashioned arcade game turned into a website interface. The concept is ingenious, with the arcade buttons as social media buttons, and the careers link in the top left is a ticket that actually slides out of the slot when you hover over it. The restaurant's promotions and important information are displayed on the game screen. The entire design has a retro video game vibe that just works, while being thematically irrelevant to a Tex-Mex restaurant.

Figure 5.3. Tijuana Flats breaks the mold of convention

Is it appealing?

Images that are aesthetically or emotionally appealing can be a very efficient hook for attention and emphasis. The issue is that beauty and attractiveness are different for everyone. Depending on the subject matter and target audience of the site you're designing, an appealing image might be a portrait of a mother and her child, a panoramic cityscape, or an adorable cartoon mascot.

Appealing images are especially important for sites dealing with restaurants, recipes, and catering. If the food seen on the website fails to make your mouth water, customers will avoid eating,

---

[2] http://www.tijuanaflats.com/

cooking, or ordering it. The images on the Olivia Restaurant site[3], seen in Figure 5.4, are amazing. They create an atmosphere that makes you want to get in the car and head for the nearest location. An image like this doesn't just express the idea of a great restaurant, but also suggests a great experience awaits you there. The chef doesn't just look like a regular old cook, he looks like an artisan, with amazing craftsmanship.

Figure 5.4. *Olivia Restaurant*: amazing restaurant photography

I realize that relevancy, interest, and appeal are all very subjective, but sometimes subjectivity and artistic license are appropriate. If you think it's a good image for the project, run with it. Generally speaking, I'd avoid monsters, slime, and aliens in most websites, but as we've seen above, given the right client and target audience, it may be a valid design direction. For every image you choose for a design, you need to be able to answer "yes" to at least two of the questions above. Why not all three? Well, sometimes it's fun to toss in an appealing and interesting image that has nothing to do with your content. You know, like a bunch of birds carrying a whale in a net (the famous Twitter "fail whale", shown in Figure 5.5).

---

[3] http://oliviarestauranter.no/

Figure 5.5. Twitter's "fail whale"

Legitimate Image Sources

So where does one acquire interesting, appealing, and relevant imagery to use for a website project? You basically have three options: create it yourself, purchase stock images, or hire a professional. The approach you take will depend on the budget and needs of your client, as well as your own skills.

Take It or Make It

For me, taking pictures with my own camera or creating my own illustrations is usually a win/win situation. If local clients need pictures to use on their websites, it gives me a chance to escape the office and do something different for a change. I've had the opportunity to take pictures of products, restaurants, a factory, apartments, a martial arts studio, storefronts—I was even able to ride around in a golf cart to take pictures of a golf course one morning, all while I was on the clock. But it's more than just a fun outing for me. Clients usually like the idea because it shows them that I want to be involved in every step of the project. It can also cost them less than it would to contract a professional photographer.[4]

The same is usually true for illustration and animation work. Most of the time, a custom site design requires some level of illustration. For items like icons, buttons, backgrounds, basic drawings, and logos, you might consider taking a stab at fulfilling the client's needs yourself. Keep in mind that illustration doesn't necessarily have to be complex or time-consuming for the message to be communicated successfully. Take a look at the website for the agency Designzillas[5] in Figure 5.6. The cartoon dinosaur isn't necessarily complicated, but it serves as a mascot for the company, and immediately gets your attention. The bright green and yellow work well with the black background, too.

---

[4] While you may not think of yourself as a photographer, taking good photos is a skill that, like design, can be learned. A great place to start is SitePoint's *Photography for the Web* [http://www.sitepoint.com/books/photography1/].

[5] http://www.designzillas.com/

Figure 5.6. The Ferocious Designzillas Website

Occasionally, the do-it-yourself method doesn't work out for me. The illustration work the client needs might be outside my skill set, or it may be too complex for me to feel confident taking it on. If it's a particular photo the client wants, I might lack access to the subject, or the quality of the image they need may be beyond the capabilities of my equipment. In those cases, my first instinct and the next best option is to turn to stock photography and illustrations.

Stock Photography

If you're short on the time or ability to create or commission your own images, chances are that you'll find what you're looking for in a stock photo archive. These photo archives, or image banks, consist of photographs and illustrations that are created for general use, rather than a specific client or project. For a licensing fee (or sometimes for free), you can select any of these images for use in your project.

Finding the right images and photos for a design project can be a difficult task, depending on the subject matter and your budget. If your project requires pictures of animals, scenic vacation destinations, office supplies, or some random inanimate object, then you're likely to find what you're looking for easily. Every stock photo archive has these types of subjects well covered. Finding photos of people—like the girl with the unnaturally blue eyes and curiously long sleeves on the Brochure Ninjas[6] site in Figure 5.7—can be a little trickier; most stock photo sites require that the photographer submit a signed model release for any image that includes a person's face.

---

[6] http://www.brochureninjas.com/

Figure 5.7. Photos of people, like this one at Brochure Ninjas, can be more expensive

For this reason, you should expect to pay for good-quality pictures of people. Finally, if you need pictures of a product logo, current celebrity, or famous work of art, you have some work to do. Even though you may be able to find these sorts of images easily on search engines, using them for a professional project will likely require a very detailed licensing agreement.

 Always Look for Image Usage Guidelines

Even if an image is restriction-free, you should ensure that your use of the image falls within the guidelines of the site's image licensing agreement. The guidelines for each stock photography source differs, so be sure you know what these are before you start looking for images. Some galleries even restrict their images to personal and non-profit use.

The next question you must answer before you begin your quest for the perfect stock image is: how much are you willing to pay? The price of using a single stock photograph can range from zero to hundreds of dollars. As you can probably imagine, the average quality of free images is dramatically lower than those for which you'd pay. Free images can still be worth your while, though; you just might have to wade through a bunch of crummy pictures before you find what you're after. The same goes for expensive images. Just because you're willing to pay $500 for a single photo, there's no guarantee you'll receive a Ferrari instead of an early '90s Chrysler minivan with faux wood paneling. No matter what the licensing price of an image is, it all boils down to finding what you're looking for. If you can find it quickly, and at a great price, you'll have more time to spend on the design.

Three tiers of stock photography are available: free, royalty-free, and rights-managed. Let's look at each of these now.

Free Images

I'm sure you've heard the saying, "There's no such thing as a free lunch". That idiom could be applied to just about everything, and it definitely applies to the world of stock photography. Even though there are some excellent free stock images available, somebody is still paying for the equipment and the time it takes to create those images. Why would photographers do all this for free? For the same reason a talented musician might publish free MP3s, or a team of programmers might spend time on an open source project. It's what they love to do, it allows many more people to enjoy their work, and it's an opportunity for their work to be noticed.

Of all the free stock photography sources out there, the one with the largest collection of free images, and the one that I use most often, is Free Images,[7] pictured in Figure 5.8.

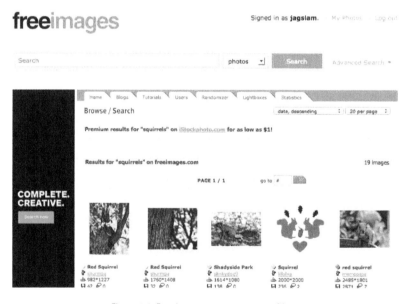

Figure 5.8. Free Images, a great source of imagery

Free Images has over 400,000 high-quality, user-submitted images. To ensure the quality and relevance of the gallery's database, site moderators check each submission before it becomes available. When you're downloading images from Free Images, be sure to check the restriction status of the image. Most images in the database are restriction-free, which means that you can use them for most personal or commercial uses.

---

[7] http://www.freeimages.com/

The size of a stock photography collection plays a big role in how useful it can be. The more photos there are for a given search term, the more likely you are to find one that's useful. Although there are many free stock photo resources online, most of them have significantly fewer images, or the images they do have cover very specific, narrow topics. One such niche site for images is Old Book Illustrations.[8] The site has a large collection of scanned artwork and illustrations, like the image in Figure 5.9, that are all old enough to be in the public domain. You can find a list of other sources for public domain images at Wikipedia's listing for public domain image resources.[9]

Gentiane jaune (*gentiana lutea*).

Figure 5.9. Image from Old Book Illustrations

If you've spent any time looking for the right stock image, you'll know that finding what you need can be a frustrating experience. Sometimes you'll spend more time searching than designing, and when it's a client project you're working on, you simply can't afford to waste time. When you're willing to pay a little for the right image, the task of finding that image becomes much easier. That's when paid stock images, which generally come in two flavors—royalty-free and rights managed—come to the fore.

Royalty-free Images

Contrary to what you might think, a royalty-free image is not available for use free of charge. The term refers to the details of the image's licensing agreement. A royalty-free image license is one that allows you to pay a single, up-front fee for an image. The payment buys you the right to use that image for other clients and projects without paying further licensing fees, known as royalties. As you can imagine, this is a popular option with designers who may need the same types of images again and again, and want to avoid the hassle of negotiating usage rights. One of the most popular places to purchase royalty-free stock photography is iStockphoto,[10] shown in Figure 5.10.

While many of the larger stock photo sites only source content from professional photographers, iStockphoto makes it easy for anyone to put their photos, illustrations, even audio or video up for sale. To maintain the quality and diversity of the iStockphoto collection, the site administrators accept only high-quality images and often reject subjects on which they already have an abundance of imagery.

---

[8] http://www.oldbookillustrations.com/
[9] http://en.wikipedia.org/wiki/Wikipedia:Public_domain_image_resources
[10] http://www.istockphoto.com/

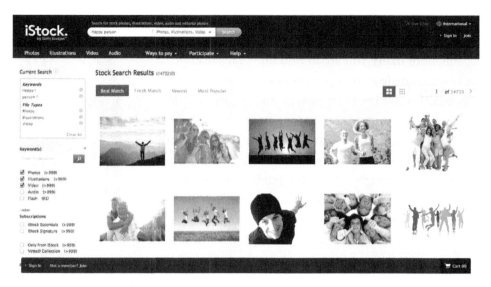

Figure 5.10. iStockphoto search for "happy person"

The reason for the difference in quality between stock imagery from Free Images and iStockphoto is quite simple. iStockphoto pays its artists; therefore, the site attracts more submissions of higher quality. Purchasing images here is based on a credit system. Once you've created an account, you can purchase a pack of credits, which is sort of like buying tickets for a carnival. The price of these credits ranges from around $1 to around $1.50 per credit; the more credits you buy, the cheaper they are. Standard images on iStockPhoto range from 2 to 25 credits, depending on the size of image you need, and some images have a higher tariff, too. I know what you're thinking: $1.50 per credit times 25 credits is $37.50 per image. On the Web, though, you typically only need one of the smaller image sizes that cost 10 credits or less. Another service that's similar to iStockphoto but slightly less expensive is Dreamstime.[11] While iStockPhoto used to be my go-to resource, I've found that I can usually find what I'm looking for in Dreamstime's collection, which also features a growing number of free images.

If you plan to download a lot of stock photography, paying by the image can become expensive, even at 2 credits apiece. An alternative to the credit-based system is to pay for a subscription service. A few stock photography providers do not sell images individually; rather, they charge a monthly subscription fee that allows you to download whatever you need. Depositphotos.com[12] and Shutterstock[13] are two such providers. Although these types of services generally cost around $100/month, they offer discounts for customers who purchase multiple months' access at a time.

Rights-managed Images

A third level of stock photography service is known as rights-managed. This type of stock photography can be quite a bit pricier than the others, as you pay a fee based on the size of your business,

---

[11] http://www.dreamstime.com/
[12] http://depositphotos.com/
[13] http://www.shutterstock.com/

the number of people who will be exposed to the image, and the amount of time for which the image will be in use. Most of the larger stock providers have rights-managed options for their exclusive images; for example, Corbis,[14] and Getty Images.[15] The photos in a rights-managed collection are usually of a professional quality.

Because the company in charge of the rights knows who's using the images and for how long, it's extremely unlikely that your client's competitor will have the exact same image on its home page that you've used for your client. With such a large pool of royalty-free images available, this may already seem improbable, but whether people notice it or not, this happens all the time. TinEye[16] is a great tool for checking how widespread the use of a particular stock image is. This browser plugin touts itself as a reverse image search engine. You simply right-click on an image that you want to research, and it searches for matches in its index of nearly two billion images. As you can see in Figure 5.11, it will even find heavily modified versions of the original image. It's important to note here that, while there are many images of female customer service representatives with microphone headsets on stock photography sites, it's a horribly overused cliché. You should think twice before using this type of image, or any picture you can conceive involving business people standing around or shaking hands. The irony here is that the ad in the TinEye sidebar includes a different picture of a headset girl. They're everywhere, I tell you!

---

[14] http://www.corbisimages.com/
[15] http://www.gettyimages.com/
[16] http://www.tineye.com/

Figure 5.11. TinEye search results for a popular iStockPhoto image

While shelling out extra money for rights-managed photography may help your clients to avoid this type of scenario, there's no real guarantee of exclusivity. If you need to, the best option is to have photos taken professionally.

Getting Professional Help

If you plan to hire a professional photographer to do your dirty work, be sure to find one who has experience with commercial photography and the type of shots you're looking for. That excellent photographer that captured your brother-in-law's tears at your cousin's wedding, for instance, may be great at portraiture and event shots, but might know nothing about architectural or product photography.

The best way to find a good commercial photographer is by word of mouth. If you know of other companies that have hired a professional photographer, ask about who they use on a regular basis, and their experience. If you don't have any references you can ask, try starting with a local professional association. If you're in the US, the American Photographic Artists website[17] is a great place to start. Many of the photographers listed in the APA database have biographies and portfolios that can give you a good idea of their capabilities.

---

[17] http://www.apanational.com/

To have an accurate handle on the costs, be very specific when writing a request for proposal. Be sure to include the details of each shot you need. State where you'd like to have the pictures taken if they're going to be done outside the photographer's studio, and be ready (with models, locations, wardrobes, and so on) to take all the pictures on the same day if possible. Most professional photographers charge by the day or half-day. Daily rates can vary quite a bit, depending on the market and the photographer's experience, but they can range from just under one thousand to several thousand dollars. Another aspect to take into consideration is the photographer's copyright and usage guidelines. Many photographers will grant full ownership of the original photographs to your client upon payment. Some will require credit if the work is used in a commercial publication. A few photographers may require that they retain exclusive rights to the pictures they take, and they'll charge per use of the photos. You should try to negotiate full ownership and usage permissions whenever possible, but keep in mind that this type of contract may cost more.

If it's a professional illustrator you'd like to hire, another resource to look into is Hire an illustrator![18] This industry index hosts over 300 artists, and makes it easy to find the person for the job by name, style, medium, or location. As with hiring a photographer, though, the best way to find the person for the job is often by word of mouth. In the past, I've helped organize a web conference here in Columbia, South Carolina called Converge SE.[19] I credit a lot of the success and personality of past years' events to the older version of the site that had illustrations of the bizarre "convergent creatures" (like Sharktopus, seen on the home page on Figure 5.12) that were drawn by Giovanni DiFeterici.

Figure 5.12. The Converge SE site, featuring Sharktopus

I've had the opportunity to meet Giovanni and many other local designers, developers, photographers, animators, videographers, and more at local user group meetups. If you live in or near a big city,

---

[18] http://hireanillustrator.com/i/
[19] http://convergese.com/

chances are there are user groups for whatever branch of the web, tech, or design industry you're interested in. These are great places to find the talent you need to complete your next project, or even to hire for your team.

No matter what sources you use for your images—whether they're from a free stock website like Free Images, or a paid professional creates them—it's ultimately your clients who should have the final say. Even though it's likely that you'll be choosing the images that you feel best represent their company, sometimes your clients will disagree with your choices. Always be ready to adapt and make changes where necessary. As long as you're creating good work and acquiring your images from legitimate sources, your hard work should pay off, and the client will be impressed.

How Not to Impress

So I've told you about a few resources where you can obtain imagery for your projects. Now it's time to talk about where *not* to source imagery from.

Google Ganking

As a web designer, you may find it inspirational to run a Google image search for topics around which you're building a website. Let's say you're building a website for a bike shop. If the owner of the shop has yet to give you any images to work with, doing an image search for mountain biking, bike races, road bikes, and other related subjects can give you a better visual understanding of the topic, and an idea about the types of images you'll want to use on the site. Usually, this type of search will return some images that would work well in your design. You might even feel the urge to save some of these images to your computer, open them up in Photoshop, and crop, resize, and modify them a little to fit your needs. This is known as **Google Ganking**, and it's a serious problem in web design. Unless the images on a website are specifically marked as being free to use or available in the public domain, you can assume that they're copyrighted by the site's owner, so you'll need permission to use them. You may think that image owners will never notice that you've ripped off their work, but you risk facing embarrassment when a cease-and-desist letter is sent to your client, or worse still, the more serious situation of a lawsuit.

The same is true for the most part with images found via a Flickr search. While most Flickr images are copyrighted by their respective owners, the service also allows uploaders to give their images one of several standard Creative Commons (CC) licenses.[20] These licenses provide a series of pre-defined rules for what you can and can't do with the licensed works. One of the license options allows images to be used for commercial purposes. Figure 5.13 shows a search for photos of chipmunks that have a license allowing commercial use. This is the same search I did on Free Images in Figure 5.8—but instead of 50 results, I received 2,423. You can see why I've seen a few resources lately that point to CC Flickr images as a great alternative to using stock photography. While it's a great image resource, it is *not* stock photography. At the bare minimum, any image you use from

---

[20] http://www.flickr.com/creativecommons/

Flickr requires attribution. If you fail to provide a credit link for every Flickr image you use, you might as well be stealing them.

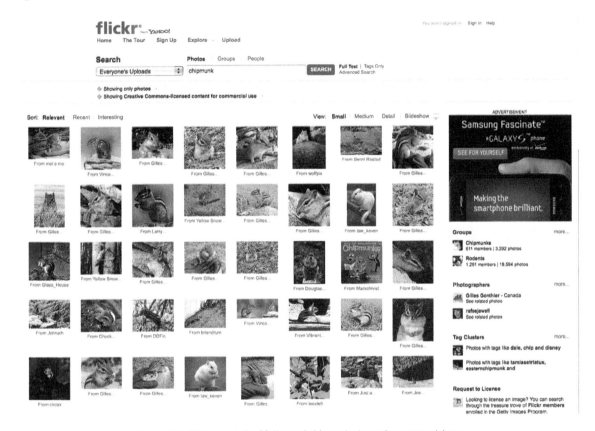

Figure 5.13. Flickr search for CC-licensed chipmunk photos for commercial use

Hotlinking

If there's anything that designers hate more than seeing their designs or images ripped off, it's seeing them ripped off by a site that's linking to the files on the designers' own servers. Usually, images for a website are placed on the same web server as the site, and are linked to in the way shown here:

```
<img src="/images/image.jpg" alt="Image Description" />
```

However, images can also be linked to from outside the website, using the full URL of the image:

```
<img src="http://www.somesite.com/images/image.jpg" alt="Image Description " />
```

Going back to my theoretical bike shop example, let's suppose I wanted to use a picture of a particular make and model of bike. Let's say I found an image of the right bike on the manufacturer's site and wanted to use it. Rather than requesting product images from the manufacturer, or even downloading the image and placing it on my client's web server, let's imagine I decide to link straight to the image on the bike manufacturer's website. This dubious practice is called **hotlinking**.

Copyright issues aside, hotlinking uses the bandwidth of the website on which the images are located. With most hosting accounts, bandwidth is limited and extra bandwidth can be expensive. So as a real-world metaphor, hotlinking is a bit like using another person's cell phone minutes to make your call. Most web professionals know that hotlinking is a big no-no, so the usual hotlinking suspects are forum users, bloggers, and MySpace users who don't know any better. So if you were unaware before, now you know better, too. Not to mention an additional problem with hotlinked images: the source of the image could pull or remove that image and replace it with something crude or embarrassing at any time.

Clipart

There are many websites that offer free, or very cheap, clipart and illustration packages. While these cheesy generic graphics may work for an internal company bulletin or do-it-yourself greeting card, they should be considered off-limits for any professional project.

Figure 5.14. Clipart could make this happen to YOU

You may think that I'm being a little harsh with that statement, but take a moment to think about it. If you go to a five-star restaurant, would you expect to be served instant mashed potatoes from a box? Of course not! You'd expect fresh ingredients, cooked from scratch. As a designer, you have an obligation to cook something up for your client that's as original as it is astonishing. While the quality and "freshness" of stock photography can be questionable as well, there's nothing worse than seeing a good design blemished by stale, clichéd clipart. If your clients ask you to use clipart or a corny animated GIF on their site, you should push back a little. Just remember that if the client has come to you for the design, it's your job to provide feedback that'll make their site look good. However, you also have to remember that, ultimately, the client is always right. Sometimes a client will force a design decision, and you'll just have to go with it. I guess some people really like their instant potatoes.

Regardless of how good a job you've done choosing images for your design, there's another critical factor to consider: presentation. When you're formatting images for use on your site, their presentation will often depend on the constraints of the layout you've chosen. The image size, for instance, may depend on the size of the rectangle you have available in your grid. As the designer, it's up to you to determine how an image will be cropped, if an image will have any framing or borders, and what types of visual effects will be applied to the image, if any.

Creative Cropping

One of the most profound impacts you can make on the presentation of an image comes from wisely choosing what should be included, and what should not. This process is known as **cropping**, and is a fundamental image manipulation technique.

At its most basic level, cropping can be used to eliminate unnecessary or unsightly details from a picture. The picture in Figure 5.15 is one that I took while wandering around with my wife in downtown Charleston, South Carolina. It's an okay picture, but the people in the immediate foreground and the power lines that run down the shady right-hand side of the street are distracting.

Figure 5.15. An unedited photo of downtown Charleston

By cropping out some of the bottom and the right side of the photo, the entire image—shown in Figure 5.15—feels less busy, more like a casual holiday shot. In the original photo, the perspective made the church steeple the focal point, but the image included too many other elements that competed for viewers' attention. With the image cropped, the steeple is still the focal point, but the pair of shoppers jumps out as a secondary focus, due, in part, to the rule of thirds I talked about in Chapter 1. Even though the steeple is no longer in the center of the composition, the perspective lines that run along the top of the buildings, the edge of the road, and even the yellow line point toward the steeple's base. Having this off-center element as the focal point of the image creates a more interesting composition, and helps to give the image a more intentional, balanced feel.

Figure 5.16. Charleston cropped

We can also crop images in unexpected ways to portray a sense of emotion, show an interesting perspective, or change the overall message of the image. In Figure 5.17, an image of a guitar player has been cropped tightly to show only the body of the guitar. This treatment highlights the sense of movement that's inherent in a musical performance, and provides a degree of anonymity that allows more people to connect with the image.

Figure 5.17. Tight cropping to give an image a sense of emotion and movement

When cropping images tightly, like the guitar image above, it's important to be aware of the overall size of the image you're working with. You may want to crop to a very detailed area of the photo and then enlarge it, but if the image's resolution is too low, the cropped image will look pixelated.[21] Fortunately, images that are used on the Web can have much lower resolutions than those used in print, but always check the quality of your final image to make sure that it isn't grainy or blurry.

Images don't always have to be contained in boxes. Many of the fun and useful ways in which we can crop photos are more creative than just trimming off the sides. The photo in Figure 5.18 is one that I took from the banks of the Saluda River. I love this picture so much in its unedited form that I made it into a background image for my computer, but let's try to think outside the box.

Figure 5.18. The Saluda River

Unconventional cropping methods can come off as amateur if they're poorly executed, but if they're done well, they can be used to create some very striking graphics. Let's say I was designing a website

---

[21] Unless, of course, you find yourself in an episode of *CSI*.

for an outdoor center that rented kayaks for use on the Saluda River. In that case, I might use a technique like the one illustrated in Figure 5.19.

Figure 5.19. River image cropped around a kayaking shape

Here, I've used a vector image of a pair of kayakers as a mask around which to crop my original Saluda River picture. In image editing software, a mask is basically a window through which you can see the image. When I laid the mask of the kayakers over the image of the river, I produced the top half of Figure 5.19. By flipping the mask vertically, and applying it to a blue-tinted duplicate of the original, I was able to create the appearance of a reflection.

Now that image might work for a kayak rental center website, but what if we were creating images for a website that promoted a regional visitor center? The center wouldn't want to limit the river as only great for kayaking. It's also a great area for swimming, hiking, and fishing. By using the text "RIVER" as a mask in Figure 5.20, I've made the image much more versatile, while establishing a fresh and creative look.

Figure 5.20. Using text as a mask to crop the Saluda River image

One final non-rectangular approach to cropping involves removing an image entirely from a scene. The part of the image that we remove is known as a **knockout**. A knocked-out image can be featured without a background, placed onto another image, or even duplicated and rotated several times to make a flower. Okay, so maybe the last example of using a knockout in Figure 5.21 is a bit far-fetched, but you have to admit that my banana flower looks fairly darn cool.

Figure 5.21. Knockout examples: bananas sans background, bananas in the sky, and a banana flower

As you can see, cropping provides endless possibilities for the production of unique images and design elements. The only limiting factors are your imagination and the ability to flesh out ideas in Photoshop.

Photoshop Adjustments

While many software packages are available to help us edit images, Adobe Photoshop has long been my tool of choice. Despite its steep price tag and learning curve, my work flow would suffer without it. It's the genuine Swiss Army knife of image-editing software packages, and the undisputed industry standard. Other tools may be cheaper, but they only have the blade, or the nail file, or maybe just the cheap plastic toothpick. Photoshop, on the other hand, slices, dices, and creates convincing watercolor-styled images in milliseconds. I'll refer to Photoshop quite often in the following discussion; however, most of the topics I'm going to talk about here are basic image adjustments that come standard (in some form or another) with just about every image-editing software on offer. I guess what I'm saying is that this section is really about image adjustments, or "photo-shopping" with a lowercase "p."

When I'm taking personal pictures with my digital camera, I usually try to think a little about composition and lighting, but as I'm no real photography pro, my photos generally don't turn out so great. Those "not so great" images often go straight to my personal photo gallery as records of places or events. If I'm taking a picture for a design project, though, these images always undergo some form of change before they're suitable for use in client work. At a minimum, the changes I'll make usually include cropping, and altering the brightness, contrast, and saturation of the photo.

Figure 5.22 is an example of a photo straight from my digital camera. It's a picture of the amazing stonework around the entrance to the Biltmore Estate in Asheville, North Carolina, that I took during a visit last summer. It's an okay photograph, but it's definitely unfit for professional use. Even as a straight content image, it has competing focal points and feels unbalanced.

Figure 5.22. Another raw photo: the entrance of the Biltmore Estate

My first step is usually to crop the image to focus on the aspects I want to show. In this case, I plan to highlight the human figure to the right of the door. As a hypothetical scenario, let's say I want to use it for the feature image in a news article about the Biltmore Estate. I like the close-up of the sculpture in Figure 5.23, but I want to find a creative way to hide the eave over its head. One way I could achieve this would be to use an image box that cuts off that part, but shows the figure popping out of the top and left-hand sides.

Figure 5.23. Initial cropping of Biltmore entrance carving

To create this effect in Photoshop, I need two image layers: one that has the isolated stone figure, and another that has the background. I start out by duplicating my image several times, making sure to keep one completely unedited version in case I need to go back to step one. For the top layer, I carefully knocked out the figure by zooming in and using the polygonal lasso tool to select the perimeter of the figure and cut off the excess. To create the background image, I used the rounded rectangle tool to create a mask of the area I wanted to show, then dragged the mask onto my background box layer.

Figure 5.24. The Biltmore image double-cropped with two layers

The resulting image in Figure 5.24 looks quite good, but it could still use some adjustments. The first issue I have is that the grimy areas on the figure's shoulders and its shield are a bit unsightly. I'm not going to eliminate that completely, but I can take some steps to reduce the contrast in those areas. The tools for this job are the Dodge and Burn tools. The Dodge tool is a brush-like tool that actually lightens the area that you click on, while the Burn tool darkens the area. By using these tools together, I can lighten the dark areas, and darken the light areas, to give the image more consistent shading and contrast.

Next, it's time to adjust the overall brightness and contrast of the two layers. Brightness and contrast are two controls that are provided by just about every image-editing software; they can be accessed in the Photoshop menu through the **Image** > **Adjustments** > **Brightness/ Contrast...** menu options. The controls are shown in Figure 5.25.

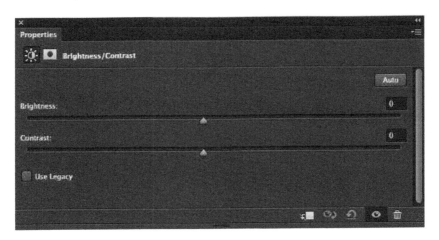

Figure 5.25. Photoshop's Brightness/Contrast controls

As we learned in Chapter 2, the brightness of an image actually refers to the overall amount of light or darkness in the image. The contrast of an image is the difference between the light and dark areas in the image. Kicking the brightness and contrast of the Biltmore figure up a few notches, and pushing the brightness and contrast of the background block down a bit, will help to give the composition a little more pop.

After I adjust the brightness and contrast, I move on to work on the hue and saturation. The Hue and Saturation controller shown in Figure 5.26 can be accessed through the **Image** > **Adjustments** > **Hue/Saturation...** menu options. The Hue control affects the overall color of the image. By moving the Hue slider up and down, you can shift the colors in the image so that it appears more blue, or red, or orange, and so on. The overall tone of this image is fine, so I don't really want to adjust its hue too much, but it's sometimes necessary to alter the hue if you want to change the overall color of an image. The Saturation slider affects how saturated the colors appear within the image. If you turn the saturation off, you'll be left with a grayscale image, but if you turn it all the way up, all the colors will be brighter and more dramatic. I want to increase the saturation in the image of the figure, and reduce the saturation of the background image. This will further extenuate the contrast, and give the image the pop that I was talking about before.

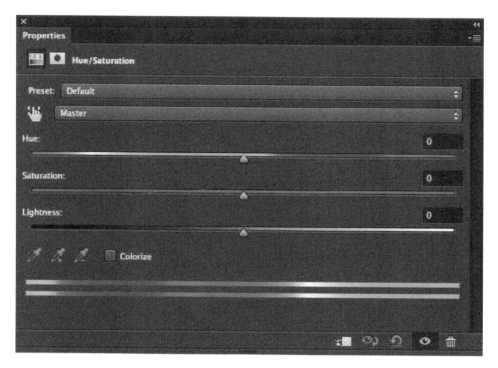

Figure 5.26. Photoshop Hue/Saturation Controls

Finally, the image is just about ready for post-
ing! Notice how the figure in Figure 5.27 stands
out from the background, and the shading is
more even than before. These subtle details
make a big difference to the overall effect of the
image. To adjust a little more of that detail, I
applied an outline stroke around the background block by accessing **Layer** > **Layer Style** >
Stroke… and giving the block an inside black
stroke.

Besides making brightness, contrast, and saturation adjustments, another way to give an image
a Photoshop face-lift is by using filters.

In photography, a **filter** is a physical attachment
for your camera lens that alters the way a photo

Figure 5.27. Final image after Photoshop tweaking

looks. These filters are used to capture richer colors, compensate for bad lighting, or make an image
feel warmer or cooler. Photoshop filters follow this basic idea, although they do much more than
a camera lens attachment. They can be used to create artistic effects, distort images, add texture,
and much more. Photoshop comes stocked with a great variety of filters. Some of these can be very
useful, and some … well, I find them less useful, but suffice to say that there's something for
everyone. For an idea of what's possible with filters, I opened a picture of some orchids and ran it
through a few of the standard filters in Photoshop. Figure 5.28 shows the results of my experiment.

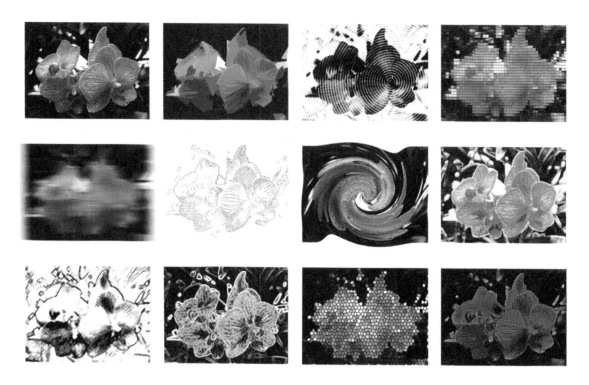

Figure 5.28. A sampling of Photoshop filters

As far as Photoshop effects go, I've only shown the tip of the iceberg here. Not even the whole tip—this quick tour has been more like a chip off the tip. There's so much that you can do within Photoshop, and my best recommendation for learning it all is to tinker. Online tutorials will accelerate that process, but there's no substitute for solid experience. Open an image and explore what each toolbar button, drop-down item, menu action, and filter can do to that image. Once you've messed up that image well enough, open another one and start again.

File Formats and Resolutions

No matter which photo-editing program you use, to prepare images for the Web, you'll need to know a few basics about the standard image file formats and when each should be used. Currently, three image formats are widely supported by web browsers: JPEG, GIF, and PNG. Choosing the format that's right for your image is a matter of determining which will provide the smallest file size for the highest quality image.

JPEG

JPEG (**.jpg**) is an image compression format that was developed by the Joint Photographic Experts Group specifically to store photographic images. Unlike GIF and PNG images, JPEGs can provide fairly small file sizes at 24-bit color. This makes them great for any type of photography, or graphics with heavy textures or long gradients. Although there's no limit to the number of colors the JPEG format can display, it's a lossy format that can create visual artifacts depending on how much you compress the file. When saving a **.jpg** file, you'll have to carefully consider the amount of compression you apply. As you can see in Figure 5.29, a highly compressed image might be great for page load speed, but if you go as far as I did with the rightmost strawberry, it's very unappetizing.

Figure 5.29. An image of a strawberry saved at increasingly higher levels of JPEG compression

GIF

GIF (Graphics Interchange Format) is an 8-bit format that compresses files on the basis of the number of colors in the image. Although the compression ratio of the GIF format is good, it supports a maximum of only 256 colors, and is therefore useless for photographic pages. Two nifty features of GIF are that it displays transparency (see figure Figure 5.30), and supports animation. In the late 1990s, UNISYS (the company behind the compression algorithm used in GIF images) tried to claim that GIF was a proprietary format, and charged companies royalties for any program that created GIF files. This—as well as the 256-color limitation of the format—led to the creation of the PNG format. Although the GIF format is still widely used on the Web, using PNG instead is strongly encouraged.

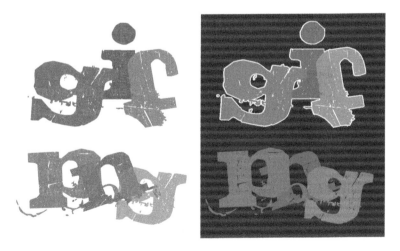

Figure 5.30. A transparent GIF and a 24-bit PNG, shown against different backgrounds

PNG

The PNG (Portable Networks Graphics) format was developed by the W3C as an alternative to GIF. The lossless compression style of the PNG algorithm works similarly to that of GIF, in that files with fewer colors end up having the smallest file sizes. PNG images can be saved in either

8-bit or 24-bit format. Both of these flavors of PNG support transparency, but transparency in 24-bit PNG images is implemented by means of an alpha channel that sits alongside the red, green, and blue channels; this means that each pixel in a PNG image can have up to 256 different levels of opacity. The effects of this difference are illustrated in Figure 5.30—notice that you can still see the background image through the PNG image, while the GIF is either completely opaque or completely transparent. 8-bit transparency is like that of the GIF in Figure 5.30—it's either on or off. Therefore, if you plan to put your transparent PNG image over a different background image or texture, you'll have to modify the image so that the opaque edges match the background. I'm hoping that by the time you read this, we're no longer coding websites for IE6, but just in case, 24-bit transparency is only supported in IE7 and up. Other than IE6, file size is another reason to consider saving your PNGs as 8-bit. The 24-bit version of an image can be several times the size of its 8-bit cousin.

Creative Image Treatments

Once you've inserted your JPEG, PNG, or GIF image into your web page, you may still find yourself a bit underwhelmed by its presentation. By default, images that are placed on a web page using an HTML `<img>` tag sit inline with the text that surrounds them. A hyperlinked image typically has a rather unattractive blue border. Not a very exciting default presentation, but that's what CSS is there for. What if you want to give an image a frame like one you might use to display a picture on your wall? What if you want an image to have a border around it that makes it look like a Polaroid picture? Perhaps you want it to have corner tabs like the ones you'd use to stick an image in a photo album. In each of these cases, you have two options: apply your desired effects directly to the photo using image-editing software, or use CSS background images and borders to style the image within your web page.

Using Images to Enhance Images

Altering an image to add borders, edge effects, and transparency may seem like minimal hassle. It only takes a few minutes in Photoshop to give a photo the look you want. But problems can arise if you have to give every image on a website the same look. And what would happen if you had to add new images or change any of the existing pics? In either case, a task that would normally involve only a minor change to your HTML, plus a second or two to copy the new photo to the web server, might take half an hour or more. On top of that, the whole point of semantic markup is to separate style from content. An image in the content of a website is just that: a piece of content.

With CSS turned off, the portfolio of graphic and web designer Wing Cheng[22] simply looks like a page full of images, as shown in Figure 5.31.

---

[22] http://wingcheng.com/

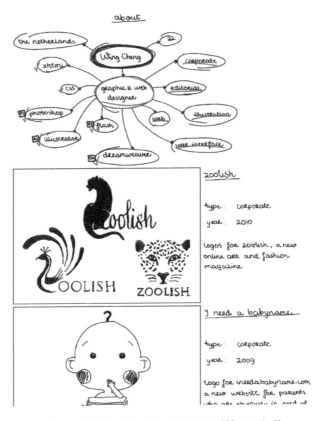

Figure 5.31. Wing Cheng's portfolio with CSS turned off

Now take a look at the site with CSS turned on in Figure 5.32. The style of Wing's portfolio is fun, whimsical, and creative. The paper pages angle in and out to give the appearance that it's a single 3D piece of paper that's accordion-folded. Each of the folds below the "about" page you see in the screenshot contains a single portfolio item. There are several items for each of the categories, and the site ends with a contact form and then the back cover of the leather sketchbook.

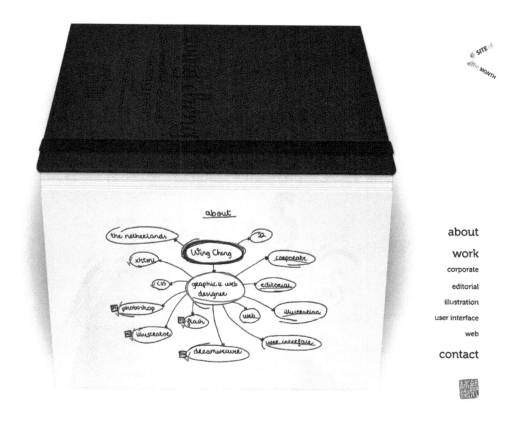

Figure 5.32. The creative portfolio of Wing Cheng

If Wing incorporated the alternating page textures into the background of each portfolio item, the file size of each image would be much larger, and the site would have taken a very long time to load. Instead, there are just two different paper textures; one angled in at the bottom and one angled out. These are applied as 24-bit PNG background images on the `div` elements that contain each portfolio item. If she wants to add a new portfolio item, she only needs to shuffle the background images in the CSS, rather than having to recreate all the images for her entire portfolio.

In this example, the portfolio images were the content, and they were enhanced by the 3D paper backgrounds placed behind them.

Using Pure CSS to Enhance Images

Applying a background or overlay is a great way to give your content images a unique and unified look. Of course, not all CSS-based image effects involve extra images. CSS borders provide myriad possible effects. As you may already know, the standard CSS2 borders have three properties—width, style, and color—which are controlled individually via the `border-width`, `border-style`, and `border-color` properties, and by the shorthand `border` property. The `border-width` and `border-color` properties are fairly self-explanatory. `border-width` sets the thickness of the border using either a CSS measurement (such as 1px or 0.5em) or a keyword (one of `thin`, `medium`, or `thick`). The `border-color` property takes a hexadecimal color value.

The `border-style` property is where the developers of CSS got their creativity on. We have eight visual styles to choose from: `dotted`, `dashed`, `solid`, `double`, `groove`, `ridge`, `inset`, and `outset`—in addition to the invisible values, `none` and `hidden`. You can see these standard styles on display in Figure 5.33.

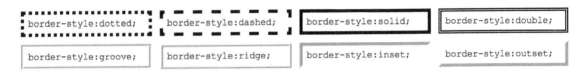

Figure 5.33. The eight visible border styles as seen in four different browsers

Figure 5.34. CSS can produce scary borders

Even with these slight inconsistencies, each style is clearly distinguished and potentially useful. I use the word "potentially" because, depending on how they're used, these borders can also be ugly. Just as good typography exists to complement text, a good border should complement the item it surrounds. Borders that are particularly large, or have a lot of color contrast, will distract viewers from the image to which you wish to draw more attention.

You can take full advantage of borders' ugly potential by specifying completely different borders for each side of a block. The ability to specify these values separately can be useful if you want a border on just one side of a block, or if you want to use different colors within the same border. But mixing different styles, colors, and thickness values around the same element or image usually only leads to trouble. As you can see from the scary monkey image in Figure 5.34, this approach can produce some fairly horrific results (though I admit that the toy itself fails to help matters).

Here's the CSS I used to create those scary borders:

```
img.uglybox {
  border-top: 20px groove #ff1100;
  border-right: 16px dotted #66ee33;
  border-bottom: 8px outset #00aaff;
  border-left: 12px double #ff00ff;
}
```

Thankfully, applying different CSS border properties to a single image doesn't have to be scary. The awesome power of borders can be used just as well for good as they can for evil. One graphic edge effect that designers often want to apply to the images in their designs is a subtle drop shadow or inset or groove to add dimension. I mentioned in Chapter 3 that CSS3 could be used to create drop shadows, but sometimes the effect you're going for is a little simpler and more subtle—like the one Claire Campbell employs on her site. In the figure below, you can see a real, working CSS digital clock. It was made by creatively manipulating CSS borders.

Figure 5.35. Subtle groove on Claire's clock

While image effects like the ones I've described in this section are useful, our ability to enhance HTML images will be greatly enhanced by some of the new features of CSS3. A great example is the final demo from Natalie Downe's *24 ways* article, "Going Nuts with CSS3 Transitions."[23] The demo for the tutorial, seen in Figure 5.36, uses CSS3 animation, drop shadow, and rotation/scale transforms to make a standard photo gallery look like a pile of Polaroid photos tossed onto a table.

[23] http://24ways.org/2009/going-nuts-with-css-transitions

Figure 5.36. Natalie Downe's CSS3 Polaroid images with captions

It's an exciting time for web design and development; the example above represents just a tiny sliver of the new styling options in CSS3. For a full breakdown of the border properties specifically, I recommend checking out Estelle Weyl's Border Properties, Values, and Browser Support[24] page at *The Standardista*. The main goal with all these display effects is to bring more attention to the images in our content, whether it's done with creative overlays, simple border properties, or new CSS3 effects. The most important point to remember is that borders and effects should enhance the images they surround, not drown them out. Avoid adding effects that call more attention to themselves than to the photo they're highlighting.

Application: The Finishing Touches

In the last chapter we nailed down the details of the different aspects of the KRG website. We'd decided on our typefaces to create a consistent, inviting atmosphere for Carrie's clients. So now it's time to refine the imagery. The main content of the site is laid out in a blog-style format, but the home page has a sliding gallery, with news, events, and product announcements that cycle through without the user ever having to scroll.

---

[24] http://www.standardista.com/css3/css3-border-properties

The most important thing about the imagery is that the individual images needed to be inviting, while evoking an emotional connection with visitors. One thing that her old site didn't do was connect on a personal level with anyone. It was mainly static text, together with an image of Carrie.

Using the right content was key in striking an emotional connection with the site visitors. To start the process of finding the right imagery, I searched my business stock photography account for images regarding pain. One of the main images on the site is of a man holding his lower back while sitting in an office atmosphere. This image should connect with anyone in the situation where they've had try and make it through the work day, even though they were in pain. Coupled with two simple lines of marketing copy, the message is highly effective.

Figure 5.37. Making an emotional connection by empathy

The three columns of text under the slider also needed some imagery to catch the eye. The first image is a reflexology illustration from a paid stock photography site. This was necessary, because it illustrates the parts of the body affected by reflexology, but in a creative, visual way.

The last two images are illustrations, created in Adobe Illustrator. One is a vector illustration of one of the machines KRG uses, shown in Figure 5.38. I used a photo for reference, but simplified it, without including any of the words, text or graphics that are usually found on the machine. Many who come to the site don't have any idea what Reflexology is, so an image of a "mysterious machine" is sure to pique interest. The graphic is simple, yet effective.

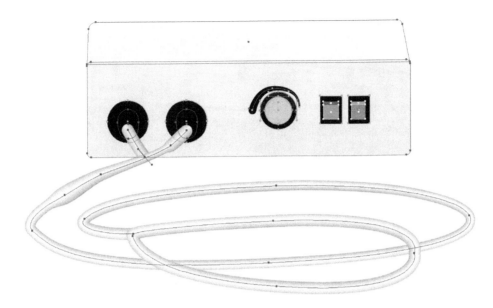

Figure 5.38. The in-progress illustration of the PEMF machine

The third image is a graphic of their thermography, or thermal imaging service. It is a good way to analyze blood flow throughout the body, and a custom graphic to illustrate this concept jumps out to the viewer against the dark green and the stark, sterile background. The position of the arms is a typical pose that's made while the test is performed.

There are a handful of important things to remember when using multiple images in a row: It's a good idea to keep them the same height, so they line up, otherwise you may run into alignment issues. Also, I saved each vector graphic as a transparent PNG, so there wouldn't be a background or box around each image. The columns are close together, and the images wouldn't have enough breathing room with their backgrounds.

Coming up with the inspiration for these images and graphics wasn't difficult. When I was in Carrie's office, I just looked around and took in all of the imagery that correlated with her business. Integrating things that I saw when I was at the location ties together her business and her website.

Figure 5.39. The final design, with images

Onward and Upward

One of the most exciting aspects about designing for the Web is the sense of community and inter-action that exists among web professionals. Whether it's on blog comments, Twitter, Dribbble,[25] or even local tech meetups, there are always talented people who are willing to share their opinions, techniques, and expertise. The design community truly is an invaluable resource—but it can also become an unnecessary crutch. I'm always looking for new sources of inspiration, and because there are so many authoritative designers out there who offer their ideas and portfolios online, it would be easy for me to find all the inspiration I need from web design alone. In and of itself, that isn't so bad, but if every web designer is getting their ideas from other web designers, eventually we'll all end up with the same designs.

While the design principles and guidelines I've discussed throughout this book can help you make aesthetically pleasing and practical design decisions, they're no substitute for character and origin-ality. The most important attributes you can bring to the design table are your own personality, experiences, and interests. These three resources should form the foundations of your design work. If every designer spent less time trying to emulate the latest design trends and more time defining their own style, the Web would be a much more interesting place. While I'd love to be able to tell you how to define your own style, I'm continually trying to learn what this is for myself. I wish you the best of luck in your future design endeavors, and hope you've found this book to be both helpful and encouraging as you kick off a career—or hobby—in web design.

---

[25] http://dribbble.com/

Lightning Source UK Ltd.
Milton Keynes UK
UKOW06f1847180914

238736UK00001B/1/P